# Dark Psychology and Mind Games

## (2 in 1 Bible)

*How to Resist Manipulation, Understand What Others Think and Influence Their Actions. 11 Proven Ways to Master Human Psychology.*

# HALBERT WARD

# TABLE OF CONTENTS

## The Bible of Dark Psychology

# The Mind Games THEY Play

# The Bible of Dark Psychology

The Only Book You'll Ever Need to Understand People's Thoughts, Actions, and How to Change Them.

## HALBERT WARD

# INTRODUCTION

Have you been wondering how to get your way with your colleagues at work, bosses, prospects, and other important people present in your life so that you can manipulate them to get your desires and progress faster in life?

Do you want to learn and implement the tactics some individuals use to get what they want from people so that you can be able to spot any attempts by other individuals to do the same to you and use it to your advantage?

If your answer is yes, read on.

You are about to learn how to use the power of dark psychology to understand people's thoughts and actions and change them to your advantage.

Persuasion has fundamental principles. What can you do to make people say yes? How do clever marketing people, sleek salespeople, and sneaky confidence tricksters manipulate people? We will take a look at the psychology behind the techniques these people use, thereby opening your eyes to the tactics of manipulation and helping you unleash the persuasive powers you have within you.

When the word "manipulation" is used, there is usually a negative connotation to it. This is the case because no individual wants others to manipulate them into doing something. Manipulation and dark psychology are used by many individuals and companies to influence lives every day whether you like it or not. So, if you have been trying to get people to do things for you and it's not working, would you like to learn more about these techniques? There may be many resources out there that may have left you confused, but this book will teach you how to use psychological manipulation.

Dark psychology is the phenomenon by which individuals use tactics of manipulation, persuasion, motivation, and coercion to achieve their desires. The tactics of dark psychology can be used for good or bad intentions, it all depends on the individual using it.

Wondering why people use psychological manipulation? People use it for a number of things. Numerous non-profits and charities use it for good. They use it to change the perspectives that people have, thereby helping them make positive changes in the world. Company managers also use psychological manipulation to influence their workers. Now imagine yourself equipped with the same knowledge about psychological manipulation that these individuals and organizations have and using it to influence people around you. Sounds good, right? This book will not only equip you with this knowledge but will also help you identify any negative manipulators present in your life.

This book introduces you to dark psychology and shows you how you can identify and protect yourself from it. It describes how you can use the skill effectively while interacting with other individuals. It explores ways individuals can control the minds of others around them through the use of simple techniques. You will be able to think more clearly and have a better mindset. It will then translate to a higher level of achievement in your goals. You will also learn how to influence other individuals to assist you in achieving your goals.

This book will help you in your personal and professional life. Emotional intelligence is important in life. You need it for your work and relationships. This book shows you ways in which to understand your emotions as well as the emotions of the people around you. When you have high emotional intelligence, you will be open to positive persuasion and be able to make other individuals feel good about themselves. Understanding your emotions will also help you learn how to become motivated and disciplined to achieve your goals.

You will learn more about body language and manipulation. When you master how to read the body language of people, you will be able to use it to your advantage. Whether it is your personal relationship or your workplace, you can use manipulation strategies to accomplish your goals. Mastering these manipulation techniques will help you in different situations in your life.

This book is an excellent guide to understanding people's thoughts and actions and how to change them using dark psychology. Manipulation differs from persuasion. You will learn how to protect yourself from manipulators and use the tactics to your advantage. When you can quickly read the body language of people, you will easily identify the positive influencers as well as the deceptive manipulators. You will learn how to influence people around you with your body language and words.

You need to understand the power of influence when it comes to changing the behavior of individuals and getting them to do what you want them to do. Understanding how individuals think will make you know how to easily get them to do what you want.

Once you master the skill of dark psychology, you will have the ability to convince people to do whatever you want them to do whenever you want them to do it. Also, you will learn how to protect your mind from other individuals, so manipulators that have evil intent can't manipulate you into doing whatever they want you to do.

People use dark psychology every day to get what they want. Corporations, politicians, and public speakers use it to get what they want from people. They use it to get votes, compliance, results, and purchases.

Body language and emotional intelligence play important roles in manipulation. Mastering these concepts will help you better gauge the individuals around you and understand what affects their actions and decisions. Understand that manipulation is not only used negatively.

It is also used to make positive changes in the lives of the people around you and in your life as well.

Dark psychology, persuasion, and manipulation are inseparable from the business world, but are you aware that you can use these skills to reconcile with people or land yourself a job, a boyfriend, a girlfriend,

and even achieve your goals?

If you are reading this book, it means you know how important it is to master the art of making people do what you want. Making people do what you want whenever you want them to do it is a skill you will need in life, especially if you are a businessman or woman. So, how can you make people do what you want them to do when you want them to do it? The solution to this is that you need to be able to read their minds and manipulate them.

The word manipulation has been tagged as something negatively inclined. But on the contrary, it can be used positively. Manipulation is when you make individuals do what you want whether they are doing it willingly or unwillingly. People do not usually wake up in the morning, to browse the internet hoping to purchase something. But the truth is, many people actually end up buying things they never intended to believe in the first place.

When you solve a problem for your audience, you are simply manipulating your audience to achieve your own goal by solving their problem. Your audience gets the solution to their problem, and you make your profit.

Studies show that a large percentage of job seekers also use dark psychology during the interview stage to land their jobs. Job seekers don't mention how often they were caught dozing off at work, and they never say how often they went to their previous workplace late. They usually don't disclose during interviews the main reason they were sacked from the job they were previously doing. Don't people often do this? Manipulating interviewers into seeing them as the perfect candidates for the job is something many job seekers do. But job seekers, influencers, advertisers, and many others do not call themselves manipulators, do they? And it's not surprising that they don't. Although manipulation alters people's views, behaviors, and even goals, you can use the techniques of dark psychology to further your interests.

Dark psychology is commonly used today. This book gives you an

excellent introduction to the world of dark psychology and manipulation. You will discover that these tactics are used more often than you are aware of. Mastering these techniques will give you an advantage in both your personal as well as your professional life.

# CHAPTER ONE:
## Understanding Dark Psychology

Dark psychology can be used for good and evil purposes. It is capable of revealing much about the nature of humans and is used to describe the study of the human mind's dark characteristics. It is a study of how individuals use persuasion and manipulation to achieve their goals. Once an individual knows how to use dark psychology, it can be a powerful tool.

Dark psychology involves discovering the human mind's weaknesses and exploiting them. Practitioners of dark psychology understand how individuals think and feel and are able to manipulate individuals to do what they want them to do. Every human has the potential to victimize other people. While many control themselves and restrain this tendency, some others don't do that and end up acting upon their impulses.

Dark psychology involves coercion, deception, persuasion, and other strategies to influence people's emotions, thoughts, and behaviors without their awareness or consent. It is often related to criminal activities such as scams, fraud, terrorism, and abuse, but it can be used in everyday situations such as work, relationships, and politics.

Dark Psychology has been in existence since ancient times when individuals used superstition, suggestion, and hypnosis to control others. In the twentieth century, more sophisticated techniques have been developed for influencing and manipulating people as a result of the study of psychology. Dark Psychology has become more prevalent as a result of propaganda, advertising, and social media. Individuals, organizations, and groups can use these tactics, which range from subtle manipulation to overt coercion, to achieve their goals. When the wrong person uses dark psychology, it can be harmful and have serious consequences for both the individual being manipulated and the manipulator. Dark psychology includes every type of behavior, from self-destructive behaviors and manipulation to serial killers and criminals. People use this technique for a variety of reasons. Some individuals use it to achieve nefarious ends, and some others use it for more beneficial purposes. For example, therapists can help patients overcome their anxieties and fears by using techniques of dark psychology. Also, police officers may obtain convictions for criminals by using techniques of dark psychology.

Individuals in positions of authority often manipulate people around them through the use of manipulation and dark psychology techniques. For example, a politician with a troubled image could use techniques of dark psychology to influence the media to present spotless images of them to the public.

A salesman or woman can convince people to buy products they don't need by using manipulative tactics. A boss could control his employees and make them do what he wants them to do by using psychological tricks. These are examples of different individuals who might employ dark psychology tactics, but you need to remember that these tactics could be used on anyone.

Dark psychology techniques are used in society and culture to manipulate media coverage, influence public opinion, and shape political outcomes. Techniques such as misinformation, fake news, and propaganda are used to manipulate the attitudes and beliefs of individuals. The techniques can lead to conflict, division, and increased polarization. They are also capable of eroding democratic values and undermining trust in institutions. Examples of dark psychology include the spread of fake news during the time of elections, as well as the use of psychological techniques in marketing and advertising.

While manipulation and dark psychology may be considered illegal, some professions use these tactics to their advantage. For example, law enforcement officers often collect information on criminals through dark psychology. Also, dark psychology is used to study how the human mind works and to help people overcome challenges. There are benefits you can get from understanding more about dark psychology and how to use it. Once you know how it works, you will be able to use it correctly when you find yourself in a situation that requires you to employ the strategies.

Dark psychology uses psychological principles in ways that benefit the wrongdoer and harm individuals. It involves coercion, control, manipulation, and, often, restricting the power and freedom of the individual on the receiving end. Psychological strategies are used to achieve one's desires at the expense of other people. Certain dark psychology tactics can be used to convince, persuade, and influence other people's thought patterns and minds, but the tactics won't work for every individual. Dark psychology works within the boundaries of logic and is not a sort of sorcery.

A key goal of dark psychology is to use social manipulation for social situations. Its goal is to benefit the dark psychologist regardless of how hurtful it is to the victims of the dark psychologist. Dark psychology involves influencing an individual's ideas without resorting to force or natural persuasive methods by using a set of characteristics.

Operant training is used to hack an individual's psyche and make them interested in the idea or information that is being presented to them. This means that the individual's behavior changes as a result of external causes. Mental conditioning and repetition affect a sensitive individual's way of processing information. This means that it will be possible for the same manipulator to manipulate them in the future.

In this book, we will delve deeper into dark psychology and its techniques. We will also discuss how it is applied in various contexts. It involves the art of manipulating and influencing people to serve the interests of the manipulator. It is important to emphasize that these techniques are about psychological manipulation but not about mind control. To better understand dark psychology and its techniques, you need first to understand your emotions and the emotions of others. The subsequent chapter will teach you this.

# CHAPTER TWO:
## Understanding Emotions

Do you enjoy connecting with people? The ability to identify emotions and understand both your emotions and other people's emotions is referred to as emotional intelligence. Studies have shown that emotional intelligence is a valuable and rare asset that can help you develop relationships, improve job satisfaction, and defuse conflict.

Emotions can impact our thoughts and behavior. Your daily emotions have the ability to influence both the small and big decisions you make about your life and can compel you to take action. Emotions can last long, such as sadness resulting from the end of a relationship, and they can be short-lived, for example, when you are briefly annoyed at a colleague at work. But what causes us to experience emotions? What role do emotions play in our lives? Where do they originate from?

We need to understand emotion's three components to understand emotions truly. Each of the elements can play a role in the purpose and function of your emotional responses. They include the subjective component, the physiological component, and the expressive component. The subjective component has to do with how a person experiences the emotion, the physiological component has to do with how the person's body reacts to the emotion, and the expressive component involves the person's actions in response to the emotion.

## Emotions do the following:

### Emotions keep you from danger
Emotions allow both humans and other animals to reproduce and survive. It is important for safety and survival. Your emotions will tell you when danger is on the way, making you avoid it. Emotions can

also get you ready to take action. The amygdala is what triggers the emotional responses that make your body get ready to handle things like anger and fear. This can trigger the body's fight-or-flight response and this results in physiological responses that make the body ready to flee to safety or stay back and face the danger. Emotions play a major role by causing you to quickly take action to increase your chances of success and survival.

## Emotions help people understand how you are feeling

When you are having interactions with people, you need to help them understand how you are feeling. You can give clues that involve emotional expression where you use body language like different facial expressions that reflect the emotions you are experiencing. Sometimes, you might also need to directly state how you feel for people to understand your feelings.

When you tell your family members or friends that you are feeling frightened, sad, happy, or excited, you provide them with important information to help them take action. Studies show that individuals experience positive emotions more frequently than they experience negative emotions.

Emotions can be a source of motivation. When you have to write a difficult exam, it might get you so worried to the point that you are afraid you will not write it well and the results will negatively affect your final grade in school. The emotional responses might increase your likelihood of studying hard. When you experience a specific emotion, you can be motivated to do something that will help you get a good grade. To reduce the chances of facing negative emotions and enhance the likelihood of experiencing positive emotions, you tend to engage in specific actions. For instance, look for hobbies or activities that give you a sense of excitement, contentment, and happiness. And you would probably stay away from situations that might bore you, make you sad, or give you anxiety. Emotions make you more likely to take action. Anger can make you confront the source of an issue.

Experiencing fear can make you flee a threat, and feelings of love can make you seek out a partner.

## Emotions help you understand how others are feeling

In the same way that your emotions provide valuable information to other people, a wealth of social information is also given by the emotional expressions of the people around you. Social communication cannot be neglected in your relationships and daily life. It is an important part of life, and having the ability to react to other people's emotions and being able to interpret them is important.

It allows you to respond appropriately and develop more meaningful and deeper relationships with your family members, loved ones, and friends. It also gives you the opportunity to communicate effectively in different social situations, from managing an employee who is hotheaded to handling an angry customer.

Understanding other people's emotional displays helps us clearly understand the best response we can give in a particular situation.

## Emotions have a major influence on your decisions

Your emotions can have an impact on the decisions you make, from which political candidates you decide to vote for during elections to what you choose to have for lunch. Studies have also shown that a reduced ability to make good decisions is experienced by individuals who have certain brain damage types that affect their ability to experience emotions.

Even in cases where you believe that rationality and pure logic guide your decisions, emotions play a major role. Emotional intelligence, which is your ability to understand your emotions and manage them, plays a key role in decision-making. Studies have shown that feeling anger or joy makes people quickly take action, feeling disgusted causes individuals to become more likely to do away with their belongings. Fear is capable of increasing perceptions of risk.

## Strategies for Changing Someone's Mind

Have you ever engaged in a heated argument that initially started as a result of an attempt at a civil discussion about a situation, but led to insults? Many people have found themselves in such situations. Though you might have the feeling of satisfaction in the moment when you hurl derogatory insults at someone, it will never help them see things from your point of view. It is important to focus on compassion and curiosity and to be clear that you don't look down on the person you are talking to or think the person is the enemy.

More happiness and collaboration are possible if people can learn to communicate better with each other. It is important to approach conversations that we consider hard more effectively. Learning how to have a good conversation when different points of view arise is vital. The attempt can be made more effective by some strategies.

## You can use these research-backed strategies actually to change a person's mind:

### Practice listening with empathy

No matter what the person you are having a conversation with says, it's important to listen with empathy and non-judgmentally.

Suppose you tell the person that they are gullible, stupid, or should be ashamed. In that case, it will cause problems and ruin the possibility of having a conversation that would actually make the person reevaluate the matter or change their mind.

Studies show that empathizing with the individuals you disagree with may increase your political arguments' persuasiveness. When you use terms such as, I understand, we all want, and I agree with you, it can show empathy. If you see that you are running low on empathy, you can get it back up by first picturing the individual you are having a conversation with when they were a little child. Then think about some dream the person has that you support or one positive moment you have experienced with the individual.

## Stay calm and open to learning

You need to enter a conversation with the right mindset. This entails striving to stay calm and willing to learn. If you know that you might snap since you are fired up, leave the issue and revisit it at another time.

Disclose any vulnerability or nervousness to the person you are having a conversation with. We often tend to want to hide our vulnerabilities or nervousness, but owning up to it can be helpful as it helps to soften people.

Avoid assuming that the individual you are talking to doesn't like you, even if you don't have the same views as them. If you begin a conversation with someone thinking that they don't want to listen to you and they hate your guts, the conversation will not go smoothly. Studies show that one powerful way to reduce partisan animosity is to correct that single misconception that the other person doesn't hate you as much as you initially thought.

## The following exercises can help you open up your heart and create the right environment for a hard conversation:

### Don't just use facts, but tell stories

Talking to a person and only firing facts at them is not often very effective. You need to share narratives and personal experiences as they will be more likely to understand what you are saying and it will be more effective.

When you connect on a human level and share your experiences, the effectiveness is higher than when you are simply arguing. People usually think that they need to argue aggressively to get their point across, but that is often ineffective.

A person can easily refute facts, but it is more difficult to refute experiences. That is why asking questions about an individual's personal experiences can be helpful. This is more helpful than their beliefs that shape their point of view, and you should avoid attacking them. It is possible if you are talking to a person who doesn't like to vote, and you are trying to change their mind about it. The person might be arguing that politicians never listen. Instead of directly telling them that they are wrong, you can share a story from your life about a time when you also felt like politicians didn't listen to what you said. This will help to form a connection with your conversation partner as they will feel like you are on their side. You can then share another story with them and talk about an experience that showed you that politicians actually listen, and how you got to know that they do. When you share stories during conversations, it encourages your conversation partner to open up and builds trust, while widening perspectives.

## Look for a common ground

If you are attempting to change the mind of someone, you can't make the conversation in such a way that you keep correcting them. You have to connect with the person. You can start the conversation by looking for something that you and the person agree on.

If someone says that people need to stop the protests against police, for instance, you could agree with the person that there are definitely good police officers. This strategy entails that you agree to the point that you can with something their statement contains, even if you don't agree with the entire statement. You need to agree with them before challenging them. This strategy can make people keep an open mindset even before you say the new things you want to invite them to agree about.

## Keep the door open to introspection

Many individuals have strong feelings about divisive issues but they never take the time to catalog the particular reasons why. You can create space for this individual actually to form their first opinion on the issue.

For instance, you might begin by asking a person a question using a scale of 1 to 10, about how strongly they feel about a particular topic. If the individual responds with a 6. You can ask them, "Why not a 5 or a 10?" When you ask that follow-up question, they will often pause and give you a well-articulated response. The individual you are having a conversation with might discover that they don't have opinions that are as strong as they had initially thought, and that room still exists for flexibility.

You can create a space where you say to the person, "I think you are a reasonable and rational person. I think we share similar views on a lot of the world's problems. I'm wondering why we do not agree on this particular issue, and I am seeking your permission to perform further investigation on the issue together."

## Know when to step away

There are some conversations that will turn into arguments. If the individual you are having a conversation with insults you, you can switch things up and tell them you wanted to go back to something before they said something else, and then you can rewind the conversation you were having. It is fine to step away if things start to get out of hand. Take a break from the conversation. You can come up with an excuse of going to the restroom, and take some time to compose yourself before making up your mind whether or not to continue the conversation and how to continue it.

## Set boundaries if you are online

You will find many annoying and long-winded posts and comments on social media. Productive and non-productive conversations alike happen there. People are usually anonymous online and you can't see their faces, so it is not hard to misconstrue their intentions and words.

You need to learn how to communicate more persuasively and productively, and online platforms can be one of the most fruitful places to do this.

# You can do the following:

## Politely set boundaries

Frame the request in a polite manner. You can say, "I want us to have this conversation, but it can't go smoothly if you question my motives or call me names. Can we come to an agreement to try to understand each other's perspective and treat each other with respect?" When you talk like this, it works most of the time.

## Be human

Users of social media often forget that the people they are talking to on social media are real people, not robots that do not have feelings. When joining a conversation on social media, it's polite to introduce yourself and express pleasure in meeting others. This will help to change their orientation and put them into a different script.

## Stay detached from the outcome

Have you ever watched someone trying to catch a butterfly in their hands? The wind that they create reaching for the butterfly often pushes the butterfly away.

The risks are the same when you are pushing the person you are having a conversation with too hard. Instead, you need to detach yourself from the outcome. Ensure that you keep a healthy amount of detachment from it. Your mental and emotional health should not be dependent on the other individual changing their mind about something.

Understand that this is the first attempt and not the last opportunity that you will have to talk to the person. You are learning, understanding, and collecting information that will be helpful to you in the next conversation, and the following conversations.

## Issue a reminder if the boundaries you have set are crossed

Someone might forget to follow the rules of the conversation when they get so caught up in rapid-fire replies. When this happens, you can let them know about it and give them another chance.

### If the individual's problematic behavior remains, mute or block them
If you have to cut anybody off if the conversation is getting abusive, do not feel bad about it. Tell them that you are cutting them off and let them know why you are doing it. Also, tell them that you are leaving the door open and they are welcome back if they become ready to converse in a productive way.

# Recognizing Emotional Manipulation

Emotional manipulators use tactics such as twisting facts and bullying to exploit a relationship to their own benefit. Setting boundaries can help you in this situation. Emotional manipulators often seize power in a relationship through the use of mind games. Their goal is to control the other individual through the use of that power.

A relationship that is healthy is based on mutual respect, understanding, and trust. This is true of both professional and personal relationships. Sometimes, individuals exploit these elements of a relationship for their own benefit. It can be hard to identify the signs of emotional manipulation, as they can be subtle. They are usually difficult to identify, especially when you are the one experiencing the emotional manipulation. That does not make it your fault. No individual deserves to be emotionally manipulated. When you learn to recognize the emotional manipulation, you can put an end to it. Your sanity and self-esteem will also be protected.

## Here are some common forms of emotional manipulation:

## They use your weaknesses against you

They can use your weak spots against you when they know what they are. They may say and do things that are meant to upset you and leave you feeling vulnerable.

For instance, "You have always said that you would never want your children to grow up in a broken home. See what you are putting them through now." "This is a difficult audience. I would be scared if I was in your position."

## They share too much too quickly to get close

Emotional manipulators may share their vulnerabilities and darkest secrets with someone too quickly to get close to them. This means that they skip a few steps in the early phase of a relationship. What they are doing with this tactic is to make you feel special to the point that you relax and divulge your secrets. These sensitivities can be used against you later.

For instance, "No one has ever shared their vision with me in the manner you have. I feel like we are meant to work on this together." I feel like we share a really deep connection. This has never happened to me before."

They make you feel guilty for your feelings

If you are sad, an individual who is manipulating you may try to accuse you of being unreasonable and make you feel guilty for feeling sad. The individual may accuse you of not being adequately invested.

For instance, "I couldn't accept that job. I would like to stay close to my children." "You would never question my decision if you really cared about me."

They may also talk about you to your colleagues behind your back.

For instance, "I would have loved to discuss this with you, but I am aware you are busy." "Since we are not very close, I thought it would be better if another individual said it to you."

## They may communicate with you through people around you

They are passive-aggressive and may sidestep confrontation. Rather than communicating with you directly, they may communicate with you through the individuals around you, like your friends.

They always appear too calm, especially during periods of crisis

Manipulative people usually react in an opposite manner to the individual they are manipulating. This happens especially in situations that are emotionally charged so that they can use your reaction or response to make you feel sensitive. What happens is that you check your reaction and theirs and then come to the conclusion that you were the person out of line.

For instance, "I wanted to keep quiet about it, but you appeared to be a little out of control." You saw that every other person was quiet and calm. You were just too upset."

## They use silent treatment to gain control over you

They do not respond to your direct messages, calls, or emails. They make you feel guilty for the wrong behavior they have displayed and use silence to gain control.

## They use ultimatums or guilt trips

When a fight or disagreement is going on, a manipulative individual will try to put you in a difficult spot by making dramatic statements. They will aim to elicit an apology by using inflammatory statements to target emotional weaknesses.

For instance, "If you cannot be available next weekend, I think it represents your level of dedication to this project." "If you break up with me, I don't deserve to live."

## They make you begin to question your sanity

Gaslighting is when someone tries to make you believe that your experience and instincts can no longer be trusted. It is a method of manipulation where you are made to believe that you are only imagining when those things actually happened. You are made to lose a sense of reality.

For instance, "I did not come late. You just did not remember what time I said I would come there." Everybody knows this doesn't work that way."

## They do or say something and then completely deny it later

They use this technique to make you doubt yourself and question your memory of what happened. When you start having doubts about what actually happened, they can blame the issue on you, thereby making you feel that you are the cause of the problem.

For instance, "I never told you that. You are starting to imagine things" "I wouldn't commit to doing that. You know I have too many commitments."

You may not easily realize that you are being emotionally manipulated, and it may take a long time before you find out. The signs of emotional manipulation are subtle, and these signs usually evolve with time.

But you need to trust your instincts if you think that you are being emotionally manipulated. Apologize for what you have done to contribute to it and then move on. You may not even get an apology, but that should not bother you. Accept your part and then don't bring up the other accusations.

Ensure that you don't try to play this game and beat them at it. Instead, you must learn to recognize the strategies used for it as you will be able to properly get your responses ready.

Ensure that you set boundaries. When an individual who is manipulative discovers that they are starting to lose control, their desperation may increase. At this point, you need to make some difficult decisions. Consider cutting the person out of your life completely if you don't have to be close to them. If the individual is someone you work closely with or live with, it will be helpful to learn techniques that you will use for managing them.

Seeking guidance from a counselor or therapist will be helpful as they will guide you on how to manage the situation. They can help to open your eyes and you will be able to recognize dangerous patterns. They can then show you appropriate ways to confront the particular behavior and stop it. It is also helpful to get a trusted family member or friend to help you identify the particular behavior and then you can enforce boundaries.

Nobody deserves to be treated in this way by another individual. Emotional manipulation is capable of having a long-lasting effect on an individual even if it doesn't leave physical scars. Understand that anyone can heal from this and also learn and grow from it.

# Importance of Emotional Intelligence

We all know that it is not individuals who are the smartest that are the most fulfilled or most successful in life. You may have seen individuals who are academically brilliant but are not successful in their personal relationships, are not successful at work, and are socially inept. Your intelligence quotient (IQ) or intellectual ability is not all that is needed to achieve success in life. Although a person's IQ can help them get into college, their EQ is what will make them successfully manage their emotions and stress during their final exams. EQ and IQ are both important.

## The following areas of your life can be affected by emotional intelligence:

### Your social intelligence and relationships
When you are in tune with your emotions, it connects you to other individuals and the world around you. You are able to reduce stress,

recognize friends from foes, use social communication to balance your nervous system, measure another individual's interest in you, and feel happy and loved with social intelligence. When you have a better understanding of your emotions and master how to control them, it will be easier for you to express your feelings and understand other people's feelings. This helps you to build stronger relationships both in your personal life and at work as it increases effective communication.

## Your physical and mental health
If you find it hard to control your emotions, your stress is probably not being managed as well. This can cause serious health issues. When stress is not properly controlled, it can increase blood pressure, contribute to infertility, suppress the immune system, speed up the process of aging, and increase a person's risk of having a heart attack and stroke. An individual needs to first learn how to manage stress if they want to improve their emotional intelligence.

When emotions are uncontrolled and you are stressed, your mental health can be affected, making you vulnerable to depression and anxiety. If you find it difficult to understand, manage your emotions, or get comfortable with people, it will be hard for you to build strong relationships. This has the ability to leave you feeling isolated and further worsen any mental health issues.

## Your work or school performance
High emotional intelligence has the ability to help you motivate and lead people, navigate the complexities of the workplace, and become successful in your career. Many companies employ EQ testing before hiring for jobs as they consider emotional intelligence as important as technical ability.

# Increasing Emotional Intelligence
An individual's emotional intelligence, which is also referred to as

their EQ or emotional quotient is the ability of the individual to understand their emotions and use the emotions in a variety of positive ways to empathize with others, communicate effectively, defuse conflict, relieve stress, and overcome challenges. It is helpful in building stronger relationships and helps people achieve their personal and career goals and achieve success at work and school. It has the ability to help individuals connect with their feelings, make informed decisions about what they are mainly concerned about, and take action.

EQ is as important as IQ when it comes to success and happiness in life. When you boost your emotional intelligence, you will easily form stronger relationships, and accomplish your goals.

You can learn the skills that make people have emotional intelligence at any time you want. However, you need to remember that learning about EQ and using that knowledge in your life are two different things. Although you are aware that you should do a particular thing, it doesn't always mean that you will do that thing, especially when stress overwhelms you, and this can override your good intentions. If you want to make permanent changes to your behavior such that it withstands pressure, you need to master how to overcome stress in your relationships and in the moment, in order to stay aware emotionally.

Emotional intelligence has four attributes. Self-awareness, social awareness, self-management, and relationship management are skills that will help you develop your EQ and help you manage your emotions and connect with other people.

## Here are the key skills for building emotional intelligence:

### The self-awareness attribute
The first step to developing emotional intelligence is managing stress. Your early life experience can influence your current emotional

experience and attachment style. Your ability to handle core feelings such as fear, sadness, anger, and joy depends on the steadiness and quality of your early emotional experiences. If you had a primary caretaker when you were an infant who valued and understood your emotions, there is a high probability that your emotions will be valuable in your adulthood. But, if you had confusing, threatening, or painful emotional experiences as an infant, you most likely have tried to keep yourself away from your emotions.

Having the ability to connect to your emotions and having a close moment connection with your changing emotional experience is important for understanding how your actions and thoughts are influenced by emotions.

Do you often experience feelings that flow, moving from one emotion to another as there are changes in your experiences from moment to moment?

Do physical sensations that you have in places like your chest, throat, or stomach accompany your emotions?

Do you have individual emotions and feelings, such as fear, joy, anger, and sadness, each of which can be seen in facial expressions that are subtle?

Can you experience feelings that are intense and strong enough to capture your attention and other people's attention?

Do you focus on your emotions? Do they contribute to the decisions you make?

If you are not paying attention to your emotions, you may have even turned them down. If you want to become emotionally healthy and develop your EQ, you need to reconnect to your core emotions, embrace those emotions, and be comfortable with them. Practicing mindfulness can help you achieve this.

Mindfulness involves purposely staying focused on the present moment and paying attention to it without judgment. If you are preoccupied with a thought, mindfulness helps you shift from the state of preoccupation with that thought toward a state of showing appreciation for the moment and your emotional and physical sensations and gives you a larger perspective on life. Mindfulness focuses and calms you, thereby increasing your self-awareness.

You need to first learn how to manage stress if you want to develop your emotional awareness. This will make you more comfortable reconnecting to unpleasant or strong emotions and making changes to the way you respond to and experience your feelings.

You recognize your own emotions and how those emotions affect your behavior and thoughts. You are aware of your weaknesses and your strengths. You are also confident.

## The social awareness attribute

Social awareness helps you recognize the mainly nonverbal cues other individuals are constantly using to communicate with you and interpret them. These cues help you know what is important to others, their changing emotional state, and how they are feeling.

You have empathy. You are able to understand other people's needs, emotions, and concerns, and you can recognize the power dynamics in an organization or group, you are able to feel comfortable socially, and you can pick up on emotional cues.

When similar nonverbal cues are sent out by groups of people, it makes you able to read the cues and understand the shared emotional experiences and power dynamics of the group. You are socially comfortable and empathetic. An ally of social and emotional awareness is mindfulness. The importance of mindfulness in the social process needs to be recognized to develop social awareness. After all, when you are zoning out on your phone, thinking about other things, or simply in your own head, it will be difficult for you to pick up on subtle nonverbal cues. You need to be present in the moment to be socially aware.

Although a lot of us are happy about the ability to multitask, what this means is that you won't notice the subtle emotional shifts going on in other individuals that make it easy for you to completely understand them. Your social goals will more likely progress further when you put your thoughts aside and stay focused on the interaction itself. When you are following the flow of another individual's emotional responses, it requires that you also focus on the changes taking place in your emotional experience as the process is a give-and-take process. Your self-awareness is not diminished when you pay attention to other people. When you put in effort and time to pay attention to other individuals, you will gain more understanding of your own beliefs, values, and emotional state. For instance, if hearing other people express certain views makes you uncomfortable then it has opened your eyes to something important about yourself.

## The self-management attribute

You manage your emotions in healthy ways, control impulsive behaviors and feelings, adapt to changing circumstances, and follow through on commitments that you have started.

If you want to be able to engage your EQ, you must learn how to make constructive decisions about your behavior by using your emotions. Too much stress can make you unable to control your emotions and find it difficult to act appropriately and thoughtfully.

Has there been any time in your life when you have been overwhelmed with stress? Were you able to think clearly or stay away from making an irrational decision? It must have been difficult to do this. When stress overwhelms you, your ability to properly assess your emotions and other people's emotions and to think clearly becomes compromised.

Emotions are important when it comes to telling you about yourself and other individuals, but that leads us out of our comfort zone when we are stressed. Emotions can overwhelm us, making us unable to control ourselves. When you are able to manage your stress and remain present emotionally, you can master receiving information that is upsetting without allowing it to affect your self-control and thoughts. You will easily make choices that give you the opportunity to control impulsive behaviors and feelings, take initiative, manage your emotions in healthy ways, be able to adjust to different situations, and carry out promises.

## The relationship management attribute

You know what to do to develop good relationships and maintain them. You also know how to manage conflict, work well in a team, communicate effectively, and influence and inspire others.

Your ability to recognize other people's feelings and understand their experiences helps you work well with people. Emotional awareness is important when working with people is concerned. You can successfully develop additional emotional and social skills that will help you form more fruitful, effective, and fulfilling relationships.

You need to become aware of your nonverbal communication and how effectively you use it. You may be sending nonverbal messages to people about your feelings and thoughts. The facial muscles, especially those around the forehead, nose, eyes, and mouth, help you to read other people's emotional intent and convey your own emotions without using words. The emotional area of the human brain is always on and other people won't ignore the messages it is sending even if you ignore the messages. Your relationships can be greatly improved when you start paying attention to and recognizing the nonverbal messages you are sending to other individuals.

Relieve stress with the use of play and humor. Play, laughter, and humor naturally ease stress. Your burdens are reduced and things are kept in perspective. Your nervous system is brought into balance, your stress is reduced, you calm down, your mind sharpens, and your empathy increases with laughter.

Ensure that you see conflict as an opportunity that can help you to grow closer to others. Disagreements and conflict are inevitable in relationships. Two individuals can't possibly have the same expectations, opinions, and needs every time. And having the same or different expectations, opinions, and needs, should not be a bad thing. Trust can be strengthened when conflict is resolved in constructive and healthy ways. Safety, creativity, and freedom in relationships are encouraged when conflict is not seen as punishing or threatening.

# CHAPTER THREE:
## Dark Psychology Techniques

Mind control, gaslighting, manipulation, and persuasion are some common dark psychology examples. Gaslighting involves distorting or denying reality and blaming an individual, making them doubt their own memories, perceptions, and sanity. Brainwashing, hypnosis, and cult indoctrination, which are used to change people's behaviors, values, and beliefs through intense cognitive and emotional manipulation, are all techniques of mind control.

Persuasion techniques involve convincing individuals to do something they don't intend to do by appealing to their needs, emotions, and desires. The individuals can be persuaded to join a group or buy a product even though they don't have the intention to do that.

Manipulation involves influencing the decisions and actions of individuals through the use of shame, fear, guilt, or some other negative emotions. Dark psychology works by exploiting people's biases, vulnerabilities, and cognitive limitations.

## Here are some strategies and techniques used in dark psychology:

- Social influence involves persuading individuals to adopt certain behaviors or attitudes through the use of authority, peer pressure, or conformity.

- Emotional manipulation involves influencing people's behaviors through the use of emotions such as anger, sympathy, fear, or love.

- Power and control involve shaping people's behavior through the use of rewards, threats, or punishment to assert dominance over them.

- Cognitive distortions involve shaping the perceptions and beliefs of individuals through the use of misinformation, logical fallacies, or selective attention.

- Lies and deception involve confusing and misleading people through the use of omission, half-truths, or false information.

# Persuasion Techniques

Persuasion is one technique that is often used in dark psychology to influence the decisions and behaviors of individuals. Persuasion techniques are used in interactions, personal relationships, marketing, and advertising. They are used to convince people to adopt a certain idea, belief, or behavior.

## Let us take a look at some techniques of persuasion often used in dark psychology:

### The brainwashing process.
Brainwashing involves various psychological techniques that are used to force a person to adopt a new set of values and beliefs. It is a process of indoctrination.

### The scarcity technique.
This is a technique of persuasion where a person has a high likelihood of doing a certain thing if they believe it is limited or rare.

### Influencing through subliminal messaging.
This technique is used to send hidden messages to people to influence their beliefs or behavior without their conscious awareness, and the messages are usually sent through sounds or images.

### The social proof persuasion technique.
This is a persuasion technique where a person has a high likelihood of adopting a particular behavior or belief if they notice that other individuals are adopting it.

### Influencing with hypnosis.
Hypnosis involves making people more susceptible to suggestion and influence by using a trance-like state.

### The consistency technique.
This is a technique of persuasion where a person has a high likelihood of complying with a behavior or request if it matches with their previous beliefs or actions.

### The authority technique.
Authority is a technique of persuasion where a person has a high likelihood of complying with a command or request if a perceived authority figure is issuing the command or request.

### Manipulating with mind control.
Individuals or groups often use mind control techniques to manipulate and influence people by altering their thoughts, beliefs, and perceptions. They often use the techniques to exert power over others. Subliminal messaging, brainwashing, and hypnosis are some common techniques of mind control.

### The reciprocity persuasion technique.
The reciprocity persuasion technique occurs when a person feels like they are obligated to reciprocate a gesture, so it makes them comply with a request. Reciprocity promotes relationships. And even though it exposes individuals to manipulation, it is a blessing and a curse. Sociopaths as well as other persuasive people use reciprocity. Hopefully, you will use the power of reciprocity for good. Understanding the power behind this principle is important.

Reciprocity is used by cult leaders, politicians, and many others to manipulate people and achieve their goals. These manipulators have commonalities that marketers and businesses should pay attention to. They include real or apparent conviction that they uphold the way and the truth. They include the determination to recruit other individuals by any means because they know the importance of having followers who are committed. They also include acknowledging that a little gift makes room for a large return favor because people are wired that way, and cultures also work that way.

There are people who might decide to hand out candies to people at a shopping mall during the Christmas season and then ask for donations in return. Our humanly biased response and the power of reciprocity make it possible for such people to receive donations far more than they would get if they didn't hand out any preceding gift.

Politicians use the power of reciprocity all the time. They use it with other techniques to manipulate people. They have the conviction and then they do everything possible within their power to mount an unassailable case for the way they have chosen so that their people would be logically and emotionally convinced of their action's necessity. They may acknowledge that their government has done something that was a mistake and they feel the need to atone for it with a gift. This makes the people accept the cost they are all paying for the things the government has failed to provide. The impact of the gift is powerful.

If used wisely, the principle of reciprocity can do wonders for you. It is formulated to make individuals feel a sense of obligation which makes them not follow their own decisions and then they do what favours you. This principle works whether you have good intentions or not.

Therefore, it is important that you ask yourself if you are manipulating people into making decisions that will harm them or if you are offering them something that will be valuable to them. As a person of integrity or a business owner with integrity, you have the

responsibility to ensure you are not harming people in the process.

There are some products and services that are not ready to be sold at any price, and this is the truth. If that is the kind of product or service you are intending to offer, then you need to clean up your act. There are some products and services that the right customer will find useful.

As a person who sells, you should have a system for identifying buyers who are qualified because your reputation is involved. A business that is needy will take just any customer or client, and an ethical business will not just take any client. They will be ready to turn down any client that is not a good fit for them and stick to genuine standards that they have set for qualification.

When you understand that your gift will open the door, it makes you careful about the people you are targeting. You can use takeaway offers to disarm buyers. Although you may not be destructively manipulative in the marketing pitch you use, you may not be acknowledging that your offer is not meant for everybody and letting those who won't benefit know that. Qualified buyers are convinced that your offer is genuine. Another basic human instinct is also appealed to. This instinct is the desire of humans to have what they cannot get.

Sometimes, we are manipulated by the rule of reciprocity as people usually like to do favors for those they like. You may use the rules of psychology to your advantage and it may also work against you. Once you are aware of the rules, you will be able to tell when a person is trying to use the power of psychology against you. Anybody can use the rules of psychology against you if you don't know the rules. Once they see any opportunity, they will take advantage of you. Understanding the rules will help you know more about yourself, understand your way of thinking, and protect yourself from being manipulated.

One psychological rule that we have been victims of is the rule of reciprocity. People will usually feel indebted to repay the favor if you do something for them. This is how the reciprocity rule works. We have been told that it is our obligation to return the favor when somebody gives us something. You will be forever indebted to the person if you fail to return the favor. You don't want to be forever indebted to someone, do you? Besides, returning the favor is your obligation, right?

The manipulators are aware of this and usually take advantage of this tendency of humans to return the favor at every opportunity they get. These manipulators know that people will often fall for this and they are right about that. Even individuals who are very smart often fall for the reciprocity rule. They are aware of the rules, but they still fall for it.

Because humans are innately selfish, we instantly like someone who gives us a gift or does us a favor for nothing in return. There is a high likelihood of us doing a favor for someone we like. The reciprocity rule is more than just liking a person. It involves liking a person for a favor they have done for us and feeling indebted to the person for the favor. You feel obligated to repay the person's favor. Returning the favor is what society considers good behavior. Society thrives this way. When someone no longer uses the rule of reciprocity for the greater good but to manipulate or take advantage of someone, it can become an issue.

# Tricks of Dark Psychology

### The lying trick.
Lying may work and it may not work. It is a planned deception that works in the liar's favor. It can also involve exaggeration or partial truth. The communicator may recount a fictitious version of a situation.

### The reverse psychology trick.

A person using reverse psychology advises someone to do a

particular thing one way, but they are aware the person will do that thing the other way. The manipulator intended for the person to do the opposite of what they have asked them to do.

### The love flooding trick.

An example of love flooding is when you compliment or praise someone to encourage them to do something that you want them to do. When you apply love flooding to make someone feel wonderful, it will make them more likely to assist you with something you want them to do. If you want them to help you move some stuff around in your home, they will be more likely to help you do that.

A dark manipulator also has the ability to make a person feel attached to them, thereby making them do things that they wouldn't normally do.

### The love denial trick.

Love denial includes withholding devotion and affection until you get what you want from the victim. The victim may find this very hard because they may feel that you have abandoned them and they may feel lost. When you ignore someone or give them the silent treatment until they give you what you desire, you are using this trick.

# Understanding Body Language

Body language is used to give our message more impact and reveal our true feelings. It is the nonverbal part of communication. Communication is more than words. Nonverbal cues such as posture, gestures, and tone of voice all play their part.

An example of body language is a facial expression that is relaxed and becomes a genuine smile. Also, it can be a head tilt showing that you are thinking, arm and hand movements to demonstrate directions, or an upright stance to show interest. It can also be tapping your feet restlessly or taking care to avoid an arms-crossed posture that is defensive. When you are able to read these signs, you will be able to fully understand what a person is telling you. Your awareness of people's reactions to the things that you say and do will increase. And you will know how to adjust your body language so that you can appear more approachable, engaging, and positive.

Understanding how to interpret the body language of people to understand them and communicate with them more effectively will help you greatly in your personal and professional relationships.

An individual's body language is more important than their choice of words and tone of voice when communicating their true feelings. When you are aware of people's body language, it means that you are able to pick up on unspoken reactions and emotions. Reading people's body language is important, but you can miss it if you don't know what to look out for.

So, let us take a look at the most important nonverbal clues.

## Examples of Negative Body Language

If an individual is exhibiting these negative behaviors, they will be unhappy, disinterested, and disengaged.

- If an individual has their eyes downcast or they are maintaining very little contact.
- If their arms are folded in front of their body.
- If their body is turned away from you.
- If they have tense or minimal facial expressions.
- Biting of nails, which suggests stress or insecurity.
- Fidgeting, which suggests that a person is distracted or disinterested.
- Blinking rapidly indicates concern or uncertainty.

- Locked ankles are also connected to anxious thoughts.
- Tapping/drumming fingers, which is often a sign of boredom or impatience.

When you are dealing with dissatisfied customers or people who are upset, you may encounter these negative behaviors.

When you are aware of the meaning of these signals, it can help you make adjustments to what you say as well as how you say it. When someone is not happy, you can show empathy for their unhappiness. For example, you can work to calm a situation that is heated or you can explain yourself more clearly.

If a person shows these signs during a negotiation, your focus should be on putting the person at ease and engaging their interest. Then, if the person stops displaying negative behavior, you will know that they are more open to persuasion and are ready to negotiate effectively with you.

Some types of body language show that a person is bored by what you are telling them. This might be in a one-on-one chat, a team meeting, or a presentation.

## Some popular signs of boredom include:

- Doodling or writing.
- Picking at clothes, fidgeting, or fiddling with phones and pens.
- Gazing into space, or at something else.
- Sitting slumped, with head downcast.

You can fix this by inviting the person to contribute an idea or by asking them a direct question.

# Examples of Positive Body Language

Individuals also convey positive feelings through their body language. The positive feelings can include happiness, interest, and trust. Seeing these signs lets you know that others are engaged with what you are telling them and they are at ease with the situation.

When you adopt these behaviors, you will be able to avoid sending mixed signals, convey your ideas more clearly, and support your points.

## Here is how you can use positive body language effectively:

### Making a good first impression.
Your body language plays a big role in the first impression people have of you. You can appear engaged trustworthy, calm, and confident, by doing the following:

### Avoid fiddling with your hair, touching your face, or scratching your nose.
If you are answering questions and doing this, it might be taken as a sign of dishonesty. You need to convey trustworthiness, so avoid doing any of that. Sincere smiles are infectious, reassuring, and attractive.

### Your posture should be open.
You should be relaxed and ensure that you don't slouch. Sit upright or stand upright and your hands should be placed by your sides. Ensure that you don't put your hands on your hips while standing, as this can communicate a desire to dominate and it can also communicate aggression.

### Give a firm handshake, but ensure that you don't overdo it.
It should not become aggressive, awkward, or painful for the other individual.

## Maintain eye contact for a few seconds.

When you maintain eye contact, it will help the other person know that you are engaged and sincere. Don't overdo it to avoid making it a staring contest. Hold their gaze for a few seconds at a time.

# CHAPTER FOUR:
## Dark Psychology and Hypnosis

So, you have the desire to hypnotize someone, but are not sure about how to do that? How can you successfully hypnotize someone? Well, hypnotizing someone isn't just about clicking your fingers and asking someone to sleep. There is a lot you need to understand about hypnosis.

How do you choose the person to hypnotize? You have a desire and you need someone to fulfil it. You can't hypnotize someone who doesn't want to be hypnotized. If an individual doesn't want to be hypnotized, they will most likely not go into hypnosis when you try to hypnotize them. So, you first need an individual who wants to be hypnotized. So, no matter how good you are with hypnosis, you don't have to hypnotize someone against their will.

After finding the person to hypnotize, you need to ensure that they are the right individual to hypnotize and you can safely hypnotize them. Some individuals are not as safe as others when hypnosis is involved and some others should not undergo hypnosis at all. Ensure that the individual you have chosen to hypnotize doesn't have personality disorders, dementia, psychosis, psychological disorders, brain trauma, uncontrolled epilepsy/seizures, severe clinical depression, and severe cognitive deficits/learning difficulties. Avoid hypnotizing anyone with any of the conditions we have mentioned, for their safety.

Once you have someone that you want to hypnotize, you need to find a location to use. You must have heard that a completely silent and comfortable environment is needed for hypnosis to be successful. You need to find a place where you will not have interruptions when you are starting out. You need to set up for success by ensuring comfort and fewer distractions during the process.

Once you are with the person you want to hypnotize, you can start by doing a pre-talk. This will help them relax and ensure they are comfortable before you start. An individual who is not relaxed or who has other things on their mind will probably not go into hypnosis. You can start the pre-talk by asking them what are their thoughts. You can also find out if the individual has any concerns before you start the process. It will also be helpful to ask about their previous experience as it can positively or negatively affect the hypnosis.

## The Process of Hypnosis

Progressive relaxation induction is a common method of inducing a state of hypnosis. However, there are a variety of other kinds of hypnotic induction. For progressive relaxation induction, you give the individual "suggestions" to help them relax their mind and body progressively. This can take only a few minutes and not hours. Before the hypnosis begins, you need to first consider how you will deliver the relaxing suggestions. Your voice should portray relaxation and convey confidence. So, ensure that your voice sounds relaxing and confident when you are ready to start with your hypnotic suggestions.

You can begin by asking the individual to take three deep breaths and then proceeding to ask them to close their eyes. Once the person has closed their eyes, direct suggestions can continue, which can include feeling calm, breathing slowly, and relaxing as your voice makes them feel comfortable. Repetition is important. You can use similar suggestions repeatedly and use them slightly differently sometimes. You can make suggestions that the individual starts to relax their muscles, beginning at their feet and moving up through the whole of their body. The next thing is to make suggestions that they imagine themselves going down a staircase of 15 steps, and that each step taken is making them feel more relaxed.

You need to give the individual enough time to listen to your suggestions and comply with them, so even though you may feel like rushing through the suggestions, take it slowly and give them enough time to respond. You are trying to make them feel relaxed, so you need to feel relaxed as well.

After getting the person to a relaxed state, the individual should be in a state of hypnosis. Some individuals remain light throughout the process, while others go deep into hypnosis. Once the person is hypnotized, you can then do what you want. They will respond to the suggestions you give, whether they are for entertainment or therapy. Individuals who are deeply hypnotized and responsive may be able to easily respond to hypnotic suggestions and engage in more complex therapy techniques under your direction.

It is easy to wake the individual from hypnosis. You only need to inform them that you will count from 1 to 5, and then they will wake up. You can give them suggestions to get more alert, awake, and energized. Ensure that you give the individual suggestions that will make them feel really good when they wake up.

## Controlling the Mind with Hypnosis

You can control someone's mind using mind control techniques and get them to follow your orders. Hypnosis techniques can make an individual do what you want them to do as the techniques help you hijack the conscious mind of the individual. When hypnotized, many individuals do things they have no memory of and things they wouldn't have done. Putting a person in a trance and making suggestions to them to get them to do what you want them to do is mind control. Many individuals have been victims of mind control techniques.

Hypnosis is not just a trick of showmen and magicians. It is used in the treatment of addictions. People also use it to forget about their psychological fears and overcome their bad habits. Burn victims and patients experiencing immense pain caused by grievous accidents and cancer have been treated with this technique and it has been known to reduce the intensity of their discomfort and control their pain. Studies show that it greatly reduces the feeling of pain.

People use this technique to help them easily lose weight and overcome their food cravings. Hypnosis also helps pregnant women overcome their labor pain and give birth to the baby easily. In addition to the medical uses of hypnosis, a few speculative uses also exist. Many skilled hypnotics use the techniques to persuade individuals to do what they are not even aware that they are doing. The person completely follows only the voice of the person. Many people have used hypnosis to make individuals hand over money without resistance or to sign the papers to a property. Kidnappers have even used hypnosis to hypnotize kids and take them away. Some individuals have been hypnotized into murdering someone and some have been hypnotized and sexually abused.

This means that hypnosis can be dangerous and useful at the same time. But, is it possible to use the techniques of hypnosis in your daily life to achieve your desires? Can you convince your child to stay focused on their studies, make someone fall in love with you, or make your boss at work to allow you close from work early every day? Well, it is possible to achieve things in life through the use of mind control.

You use hypnosis every day without being aware that you are even using it. This may even be happening to you when you like someone and find yourself often following them. So, if you notice that you follow your friend to go out for dinner or a movie without thinking about it when you are meant to stay at home and study for an exam you have the next day, hypnosis could be involved. If a person likes you, they may do whatever you want just to make you happy. Thus, you may have said yes to doing something you don't want to do simply because you are attracted to the person asking you to do them that favor or you like the person. This may have happened to you many times.

But what if the person is a complete stranger, like a prospective client or a salesperson? If this is the case, you need to use mind control techniques that involve mirroring the behavior of people. The answer can be found in watching the individual carefully and picking up some repetitive words or actions that they use. Ensure that you use the same actions or words during your interactions with that individual, and they will get to see the similarities you have with them, and this will make them develop a rapport with you.

## Controlling Minds through Stories

Have you noticed that individuals get engrossed when watching movies or reading a story that is interesting and try to copy the character that made the most impact in their minds? So, while having conversations with people every day, include some short anecdotes in those conversations that will make it possible to control the other person's mind. Negative sentences can even help you make someone do what you want them to do. Reverse psychology is like this. You tell the individual that they don't need to do a particular thing right now and then they go ahead and do that thing immediately. And this is actually what you want them to do.

When asking people to do something, ensure that you choose your words carefully, as individuals often imagine an image of what you said they should do. When you tell someone that they should not allow the glass case to drop, the person imagines it falling and may even imagine themselves making it fall. But if you ask them to transport it safely, chances are that they will do their best to transport it carefully.

You can try these techniques. You can learn hypnotism and get better at it over the years with practice. It is important that you know how to make an individual come out of a trance when you make them go under a trance. They should come out of trance without any negative consequences. Some hypnotics use a word, click, or clap to make an individual come out of a deep sleep or undergo a trance. You are using hypnosis to make the subconscious mind more alert than the conscious mind.

You have no idea of what the individual has stored in their subconscious mind that may be harmful to them and you as well. So, ensure that you are careful when you are trying the techniques. You can try mind control techniques that are easier in your everyday life and make your partner return home early or get a good bargain for a product from a salesperson. Just make sure that the attractive man or woman sitting opposite you in the bar doesn't hypnotize you.

## Achieving Your Goals with Self-Hypnosis

Have you watched television programs and horror films that portray hypnosis as something frightening that villains use to control the minds of helpless individuals and enslave them? You may have watched stage shows where it appears that a hypnotist used their "hypnotic powers" to make individuals say and do things these individuals would never say and do normally. So, hypnosis may appear wacky, like other mystical phenomena. Hypnosis is therapeutic and has the ability to help individuals overcome many physical, emotional, and psychological issues. When an individual is in a state of hypnosis, they are aware, in a natural state, and can come out of hypnosis when they wish to come out of it.

The hypnosis state is a state of highly focused attention with increased suggestibility. Relaxation does not always accompany hypnosis. When someone like a therapist, hypnotizes another individual, it is referred to as hetero hypnosis. This is often called hypnotherapy. Autohypnosis is when hypnosis is self-induced. This is often known as self-hypnosis.

The word hypnosis originates from "hypos," which is a Greek word, meaning sleep. Neuro-hypnotism is abbreviated. Neuro-hypnotism means the sleep of the nervous system.

However, an individual is awake when in hypnosis. They are not in a sleep state and are aware of all that is being done and said. People often use self-hypnosis to modify emotions, behavior, and attitudes. For example, many individuals deal with the daily problems of life with self-hypnosis. Self-hypnosis has the ability to help individuals develop new skills and boost their confidence. It proves beneficial for reducing anxiety and stress and can aid in overcoming habits like overeating and smoking. Sportsmen and women can use self-hypnosis to enhance their athletic performance, and hypnosis is also useful for individuals suffering from stress-related illnesses or physical pain. Before hypnosis can be used for stress-related illnesses or physical pain, a medical diagnosis has to be made and it has to be under a qualified therapist or doctor's guidance.

# Technique for Self-hypnosis

Let us take a look at an effective self-hypnosis technique. This simple technique is effective and popular and is known as eye fixation self-hypnosis. It can help you relax. We will first use it for relaxation and then add hypnotic suggestions as well as imagery. Start by going into a room where you will not be distracted and then turn off your computer, television, or phone. This will help you reduce distractions. This time is yours and you will be focusing on nothing else but your goal of self-hypnosis.

## Do the following:

### 1. Sit in a chair you are comfortable in and don't cross your legs and feet.
Ensure that you don't eat a large meal just before you start hypnosis to avoid feeling uncomfortable or bloated. Avoid lying on a bed as it will likely make you fall asleep. Sit in a comfortable chair so that you don't nod off. It is best to take off your shoes and wear clothing that

is not too tight. It is also advisable to remove any contact lenses if you wear them. Avoid crossing your legs and feet.

## 2. Fix your gaze on the ceiling and breathe deeply.

Without tilting your neck to the back or straining your neck, look for a spot on the ceiling and keep your eyes on that spot. While you fix your gaze on that spot take in a deep breath and then breathe out. Ensure that you hold it for a moment before breathing out. Silently say the suggestion "I want to sleep now, my eyes are heavy." Continue repeating this process, and allow your eyes to close and then relax. When you are saying the suggestion, say it as if you mean it. You can say it in a convincing and soothing manner.

## 3. Allow your body to relax.

Free yourself and allow your body to become loose. The next thing to do is to slowly count down from ten to zero. Tell yourself that you are getting more relaxed with each and every count. Focus on your breathing while you remain in this relaxed state for some minutes. Be aware of how your diaphragm and chest are rising and falling. Pay attention to how your body is becoming relaxed without you even doing too much to relax it. In fact, your body becomes more relaxed the less you try to relax it.

## 4. Use visualization.

Visualize an image that stands for something you desire mastery of and see yourself accomplishing your goal.

## 5. Use positive suggestions.

Say a positive suggestion like "I am calm, confident, and relaxed" three times.

Say it to yourself with conviction while visualizing for about one minute the image of what you desire. Repeat this suggestion three times and ensure that you stay in hypnosis between times and also be focused on the relaxation of your body.

## 6. Come back to the room when you are ready by counting from one to ten.

Let yourself know that you are becoming aware of your

surroundings and you will open your eyes at the count of ten. Start counting up from one to ten in an energetic way. When you get to ten, you can then open your eyes and stretch your legs and arms. Practice the technique repeatedly up to four or five times and pay attention to how you become deeply relaxed each time.

If you try this technique and discover that it doesn't make you feel as relaxed as you would like, don't give up, and don't force it. You only need to continue practicing regularly to become better at it. Sometimes, individuals will feel drowsy after hypnosis. This is harmless and only takes a few seconds. It is just similar to how you feel when you wake up from an afternoon nap. Although this is harmless, ensure that you do not operate any machinery or drive until you are fully awake.

# Post-Hypnotic Suggestions

Have you ever tried to remember a name and found yourself frustrated because you couldn't remember the name? The more you try to remember it, the harder it becomes. Then the name comes back to you later when you are relaxed. Sometimes, we block ourselves from accomplishing our goals when we try too hard. Your attitude towards self-hypnosis is what will determine if you will get better at it or not. Relax and don't set unrealistic goals. Set realistic goals and take your time. You may not be achieving results as fast as you want, but you should accept the pace at which things are going even though the results may seem small at first. Stop doubting yourself and believe you can do it. With time, you will accomplish your goal.

Hypnosis involves heightened suggestibility. When you give yourself suggestions during hypnosis, it will make a response or action take place after the hypnosis. The suggestions are known as post-hypnotic suggestions and they can make it possible for you to achieve your goals. As the years pass by, hypnotherapists have created suggestion rules.

## The rules have been summarized below. They will help you achieve success with these suggestions:

### 1. Suggestions should be in the present tense and should be phrased positively.

Many people will not react more favorably to a negatively worded suggestion as much as they would react to a positively worded one. You will have more effective suggestions when you talk about what you want to move toward and not what you want to get away from. For instance, instead of saying, "I am not scared," you can say "I am calm."

Would you rather hear something like, "Would you mind doing this?" or "Do not say you won't do this."

It is better to say "I stop drinking alcohol with ease" instead of "I will try to stop drinking alcohol" because using the word try means that you are struggling to stop drinking alcohol and finding it hard to stop. It is better for your suggestions to be phrased as though they were taking place presently. They should be in the present tense.

So, it is better to say "I am relaxed in the car" instead of "I will be relaxed when I am in the car". Or you can say, "My confidence is increasing" instead of "I will try my best to be confident".

### 2. Say the suggestions as if you mean what you are saying.

How do actors perform? Have you ever seen any of them speaking in a quiet voice and mumbling their lines on stage? The performance will not be convincing. People often repeat hypnotic suggestions silently. It is not like acting. However, when repeating the suggestions, you need to say the suggestions as if you mean what you are saying. Be confident, positive, and reassuring.

## 3. Repetition is important.

Suggestions are valuable to advertisers, which is what makes them repeat radio and television commercials regularly. Repetition is an important rule when an individual is practicing self-hypnosis. This helps to drive the point home and make positive change.

## 4. Your suggestions should be realistic and specific.

You will have more effective suggestions if they are realistic and specific. If you have the desire to improve your basketball performance, you cannot unrealistically give the suggestion "I am a world-class basketball player," unless you are truly a world champion or are about to become one. Instead, find out what specific thing you wish to improve upon when it comes to the way you play basketball. So, if your desire is to improve a specific area of your basketball playing, you would give realistic suggestions that are specific to that part. Your suggestions should be structured based on the changes you can make in yourself that are within your control and not unrealistic things, such as external events, that are not within your control. Do not give suggestions for more than one issue at once. For example, when you use the suggestion "I am confident that I can stop smoking and lose weight," you will notice that it is not really effective. Instead, pick one goal at a time and work on it, repeating suggestions that are connected to that goal. Move ahead to the next goal you have after you see results.

# Hypnosis and Imagery

Visualize the situation when you are giving yourself suggestions. Also, visualize your desired feeling and action. You can make use of your sense of hearing, touch, and smell, in addition to picturing an outcome that you desire. You can use images from your experiences and memories and also create new images. Individuals sometimes believe it is crucial to see a clear image of their goal. However, a belief that you are in line with your goal as well as a positive attitude is more important than having a clear image of your goal.

This exercise shows how effective imagery and suggestion can be.

Ensure that you avoid using it if you don't like lemons.

- Make yourself comfortable while sitting in a chair and close your eyes.
- Picture a lemon and imagine yourself cutting it into 2.
- Be aware of the lemon juice running down each lemon piece.
- Take a piece of the lemon and bite into it.

Even if you don't have a clear image of the lemon, you might still find your mouth watering and you might grimace.

## Adding Visualization and Hypnotic Suggestion To Self-Hypnosis

Jenny is due to participate in a play, but she often experiences stage fright and is worried that her performance will be less than the standard of performance that she is capable of. Jenny wants to practice self-hypnosis to increase her confidence. In self-hypnosis and results imagery, the individual visualizes him or herself performing in the way he or she desires while at the same time repeating some post-hypnotic suggestions to accomplish a goal. After Jenny puts herself into hypnosis, she visualizes herself performing on stage with ease and confidence. She repeats the post-hypnotic suggestion "I am performing with confidence and ease" three times while visualizing herself for one minute. She does the visualization two more times while she is still in hypnosis.

# Setting Your Goals for Self-Hypnosis

1. Get a book or paper and write your goals. Be specific and clear about what you want to do. Ensure that the goals you set are achievable. If the goals you have are long-term goals, you can break them down into manageable steps.

2. Prioritize achieving your goals. Decide to practice self-hypnosis every day and you will begin to see results.

3. Make a decision about the imagery you want to use. If your goal is to relax your body, visualize a beautiful scene like a park or a beach on a warm day. You can also use results imagery.

4. Write down the hypnotic suggestions you have formulated. Write out some suggestions to use for the goal that you want to accomplish. Abide by the post-hypnotic suggestions' rules. You can even create your own script that you will use.

5. Do not be too hard on yourself if you fail to accomplish a goal. Understand that failing to accomplish a goal does not make you a failure. You may need to stay persistent or even try a different approach towards the goal.

# Reducing Anxiety and Relaxing Yourself with Self-Hypnosis

The script below will help you cope with anxiety and relax. You can alter the imagery to make it align with your needs. For example, you may choose to imagine yourself in a park on a warm day instead of visualizing yourself on a beach. You can also choose to change the symbolism used to address a situation that you desire to work on. You can record the text and replay it, or get an individual to read it to you.

## You first need to become hypnotized as before by doing the following:

1. Sit in a place that is comfortable for you and then ensure that your legs and feet are uncrossed.

2. Without straining your neck or tilting your head, choose a point on the ceiling and keep your eyes on that spot. While your eyes are focused on that spot, breathe in deeply and hold it for some time as long as you feel comfortable. Then while you are breathing out, you can say the suggestion "My eyes are heavy and tired and I want to sleep. Continue repeating the process a number of times and, if your eyes are yet to close, allow them to close and relax your eyes in a closed position.

3. Repeat this script with conviction and say it silently and with conviction:

"I am giving my body the opportunity to become loose and get comfortable in the chair. I am starting to notice the place in my body where the comfort is as I continue to relax. Perhaps I experience a comfortable feeling of warmth in my fingers and hands or maybe I notice the comfort in some other part of my body. The comfort deepens with every sound I hear and every breath I take. I now start counting down from ten to zero. I become more relaxed with each count."

"I now visualize myself on a beautiful beach and feel the sun's warmth on my body and the sand's warmth under my feet. I imagine myself alone by the beachside or that other individuals are also there as I continue to relax. I listen to the waves lapping against the seashore and the sound of the sea. I feel so relaxed, secure, and calm, and I feel that I can remain by the beachside for as long as I want to. After a few minutes, I visualize myself in a field on a warm summer's day. There is a hot air balloon in the middle of the field and a basket is attached to the balloon. The basket attached to the balloon is weighed down on the ground with the use of sandbags. The hot air balloon hangs in the sky effortlessly. I imagine myself placing my fears, worries, or anxieties into the basket. I feel more relief the more I offload my fears and anxieties into the basket. It feels as if I had been carrying a great weight which has now been lifted."

"I let the sandbags go and watch as the balloon and the basket move up into the air. I experience relief as I watch the balloon going up into the air. I feel more relief as the balloon rises higher. My worries and fears appear to be more insignificant as the balloon becomes more distant. As I continue to watch the balloon becoming smaller in the distance, I say the following to myself five times:

"I am releasing my fear, worries, and anxiety."

When ready to come out of hypnosis, I count up starting from one to ten, and then open my eyes. When you engage in self-hypnosis, the suggestions you give yourself and the imagery you use are only exposed to limits from your imagination.

## You need to know the following:

- Hypnosis is used to overcome many emotional, psychological, and physical issues. It is therapeutic. It is not an unconscious state, a mystical state, or a state of sleep. When an individual is in hypnosis, they are aware and are able to come out of it when they want to. It is a harmless and natural state.

- When you want to practice self-hypnosis, ensure that you do not eat a large meal before starting the process as it can make you feel uncomfortable or bloated. Unless you want to doze, ensure that you sit in a comfortable chair and avoid lying down, as you might start feeling sleepy if you lie down. It is best to take off your shoes and loosen tight clothing. It is best to remove contact lenses if you wear them. Your legs and feet should not be crossed.

- Self-hypnosis is capable of modifying emotions, behavior, and attitudes. It can be beneficial for individuals to engage in activities that help them acquire new skills and enhance their self-assurance. It can also decrease anxiety and stress, and help individuals overcome habits such as overeating and smoking. Sportspeople also use self-hypnosis to enhance their athletic performance. It is essential to get advice from a competent therapist or a doctor before practicing self-hypnosis if you are facing any psychological or medical issues.

- Engage in self-hypnosis regularly. Take your time and relax. Even though you may seem to be achieving results slowly, you need to accept the pace. Your results may appear small initially, but you must believe in yourself and you will accomplish your goals and become successful in no time.

- Remember that failing to succeed in accomplishing a goal does not make you a failure. You may just need to stay persistent or approach the goal differently.

You can use the following post-hypnotic suggestions in your self-hypnosis and you can make them fit your needs:

*My relaxation gets deeper every time I enter into hypnosis.*

*I am getting more confident and assertive when I have conversations with my colleagues.*

*It is easy for me to stop smoking.*

*I am secure, calm, and relaxed every day.*

*I eat healthy meals three times a day.*

*Every single day I embrace and accept myself just the way I am.*

## Hypnosis and Its Dark Side

People intentionally and unintentionally use hypnosis to do good and evil things. Ethically minded hypnosis practitioners need to acknowledge the following risks and protect themselves against them.

## The intention.

The therapist's intention is important in terms of outcomes. Indeed, if a therapist sincerely wants to help someone, they can get a good result even if they are not technically hugely proficient. However, individuals who can put their egos completely aside are rare and therapists have egos too. Ego can cause a specific pitfall for some individuals who use hypnotherapy, as these individuals have discovered that they can easily put people into a trance, whereas, it appears to be a mysterious process for most people. These individuals might even have made themselves believe that immense skill is required, so it makes their egos puff up and this can negatively affect patients. Practitioners are often encouraged to use the term guided imagery instead of hypnosis for the sake of preventing misconceptions on the part of the client and the therapist.

## Taking away an individual's sense of control.

Humans have the innate need to have a sense of control over their own lives. Therapists are not the ones to make assumptions about their client's needs. It is important that the changes the therapist is guiding the client to make are in accordance with the client's goals that they have clearly established beforehand. So, even when the client is in a state of trance, the goals are clearly understood by both the therapist and the client. Therapists should also give their clients the tools to cope without them, as fast as possible. Therefore, mastering effective brief techniques is important for therapists. Therapists can also teach their clients to relax and avoid becoming reliant on recordings that the therapists provide for them or on recordings that they might provide for them. Clients can use these until therapy is no longer needed.

## Hallucinations.

When hallucination is induced, it can cause vulnerable people to have psychotic breakdowns. This is dangerous because an individual who is in a psychotic state cannot distinguish between the waking reality and the dream state as we usually do.

## False memory syndrome.

There are families who have been pulled apart as a result of false

memories of parental sexual abuse "uncovered" during therapy. Clinicians are being alerted to false memory syndrome. There are cases of people who have recalled some things in therapy that later emerged that they had been confabulating along with their therapists. So, it is important for therapists to be careful not to make suggestions that are emotionally arousing, even by asking questions, such as the possibility of abuse, childhood neglect, or that a spouse may be engaged in an affair, which their clients may dwell on and then dream about. The clients may then later recall the dream and without due evidence, give credence to it.

## Telepathy.

When therapists are seriously trying to help an individual, they often go into a deeply focused state and, at such times, there can be a confusion of ego boundaries, thereby causing harm to both client and therapist. A field of relationship is involved every time we make a connection with another individual. A lot of therapists experience telepathy when it comes to their clients. For example, if a therapist wishes to have fewer clients on a particular day or if they feel that they have low energy, their clients will usually start to call them up to postpone appointments. This often happens and is quite too astonishing to be down to chance. One experience that is common is suddenly knowing that a person who is close has died, even if the person was in good health and miles away.

## Using hypnotic words.

Political parties and cults practice hypnosis. For instance, when politicians use abstract hypnotic words like principles, values, or positive change, it forces individuals into an internal trance to attempt to search and understand what the words mean, even though no concrete examples are given by the politicians. Everybody has something that they want to change in their life. And nobody wants a change that is negative. So, using words like "progressive" or "change" by politicians is a con trick.

If you think hypnosis is harmless, you need to know that Hitler studied it after a hypnotist healed him of the hysterical blindness that he had at the end of World War 1. A strong suggestion that a psychologist gave him in a trance changed his personality. He was told that he had great personal powers and he was special. He was also told that he could use his great powers to cure himself of the blindness. This represented a post-hypnotic suggestion and vast crowds at rallies had receptive trance states induced in them by Hitler, thereby bombarding them with nominalizations that were emotionally arousing. A stylized form of arm levitation was even adopted as the Nazi salute by him.

In therapy, clients are sent on their own internal search to find meanings for strengths, creativity, inner resources, etc. through the use of abstract language with benign intentions, but remaining mindful of how unintended consequences can happen when language is used loosely as well as how power can easily be abused is important. If certain abstractions are not made concrete, overusing positive abstractions that induce trance can hinder a client from going forward. When therapists have clients that talk in abstract terms, the therapists may sometimes get entranced by the abstractions, do their own internal searches, and don't succeed when it comes to seeing past them. Getting seduced into a trance can be surprisingly easy, even when you believe that you know better.

## Destroying an individual's very essence.

When hypnotic techniques are used to help an individual access the REM state, the individual's unique essence is being tapped into. A hypnotic induction involves trespassing upon the private mental territory of some other person's essence. We should only enter this territory respectfully if we are invited, and the gate must be carefully closed when we leave the territory. Continuous use of hypnosis on a person will weaken them, as it is capable of putting out the spark of volition by increasing their openness to suggestion, and also to the suggestions of others. For this reason, it is important for therapy to be brief.

Therapy helps individuals detach and cope on their own, not depending on others. Severe cases of repeated hypnosis are capable of deranging the brain, as when ordinary people think of others as things and not as humans, and when they start acting in grotesque ways. When some people think it is acceptable to torture, kill, and rape people, it means that emotional arousal through chanting, repetition, fear, or other means has been used to hypnotize these people to make them become more suggestible. Hypnosis as well as the programming of people are used in all dangerous mass movements, once the people are emotionally aroused.

When an individual is bombarded with continuous regular hypnosis sessions, their mind can become powerless, thereby leading to mental asylum instead of gaining better control and power. A therapist cannot continue trying to bolster an individual who is psychologically damaged by telling them that they have a bright future and that they are desirable or they are talented, without any evidence at all, and doing nothing to make this actually a reality. People's spiritual and psychological development can be affected if hypnosis is used carelessly, and this can be called psychic murder.

# CHAPTER FIVE:
## Dark Psychology and Brainwashing

Brainwashing is the process whereby an individual's core values, beliefs, affiliations, and ideas are replaced, to the extent that the individual can't think critically or independently and has no control over themselves. Anyone can be brainwashed. This includes people who have been sacked from their workplace and have nothing to do, people who are suffering from an illness that needs to be cured by all means, people who have lost their loved ones through divorce or death, and people who have lost their homes and forced to start living on the streets. Even the most powerful and intelligent person can be brainwashed. You encounter brainwashing techniques every day and you can learn how to use them or avoid them. While it is unlikely that you may be deliberately targeted for brainwashing, you could be subject to some techniques related to the practice. You encounter these methods regularly and you can avoid them.

Mind control, which is also referred to as coercive persuasion, thought reform, brainwashing, thought control, or mind abuse, is a process in which a person or a group persuades other people to conform to their wishes through the use of manipulative methods, and this is often done to the detriment of the people being manipulated.

Brainwashing is a form of manipulation. It is usually associated with cults and people use it in everyday life. Brainwashing techniques are often leveraged by politicians, news networks, advertisers, and so on.

## Here are some of the most notable brainwashing techniques:

- The individual is offered a number of choices by the

manipulator, but all the choices they have offered the individual leads to the same conclusion.

- The manipulator provides the victim with information on various subjects and they provide it in constant short snippets. This makes the information overwhelming for the victim and trains them to have a short-term memory. The victim highly desires the information that the manipulator is providing due to how highly overwhelmed the victim feels.

- There is repetition of the same phrase or idea to make sure that it sticks in the individual being manipulated's brain.

- The individual is put in a heightened state through emotional manipulation, making it more difficult for them to use logic. Inducing anger and fear are among the manipulated emotions that are the most common.

# The Brainwashing Process

Someone who is trying to brainwash you will be intentional about knowing the details about your life so that they can use the information to manipulate your beliefs. They will want to know what your strengths are, who you confide in, what your weaknesses are, and who you consider important in your life and take advice from.

## Here is the process of brainwashing:

### The isolation tactic.

Isolation is the first tactic used in brainwashing someone because when your friends and family members are around you, your manipulators will not find it easy to manipulate you. The manipulator doesn't want someone with an idea that is different from theirs or a person who asks questions to first understand what the manipulator is trying to get them to do. This technique starts in the form of constantly checking where you are and who you are spending time with, or preventing you from accessing your family or friends.

## Introducing an alternative way of livelihood.

If you want to break down an individual and reshape the person in a different image, you must introduce an alternative way of their livelihood which is more attractive than the present one.

## Breaking down self-esteem.

A person is easily brainwashed when they have low self-confidence and they are in a vulnerable condition. So, when the manipulator wants to brainwash an individual, they ensure that the person is in a vulnerable condition to enable them to carry out their plans. The manipulator can easily rebuild a broken person with their own beliefs. The manipulator breaks down the person's self-esteem by employing strategies like verbal abuse, physical abuse, sleep deprivation, embarrassment, or intimidation. A manipulator will start to control everything about the person's life, starting from the time they wake up in the morning to the time they sleep.

## Blindly follow orders.

A manipulator's ultimate goal is to make the target follow their orders without asking any questions. Repeating a similar statement continuously is an effective way of controlling a person. When the same statement is repeated, it is perfect for halting the doubting thoughts. Research has shown that the repetitive and analytical parts of the mind are not interchangeable.

## Humiliation and degradation.

You get more harmed by the brainwasher when you stand up for yourself, question their ideas, or resist their demands. When you get angry, the punishment you go through is more severe than just doing what they wanted you to do in the first place. The brainwasher will often use mere words to degrade you through abuse, and they will humiliate you before friends or co-workers whenever they like. The humiliation degrades you and reduces your sense of self-worth.

## Issuing threats.

The brainwasher threatens the victim that they will leave the relationship. The abuser also uses body language to deliver the threats.

## Testing their target.

Brainwashers don't often think that they have completed their work, as there are times when their victim could start thinking for themselves again and then take back control of their life. When a brainwasher tests their target, it makes them see that they are still brainwashed and the brainwasher gets to understand how much control they have over the individual. They might ask their target to do something like a criminal act, for instance, robbing someone's store or burglarizing a home.

## Prove that they know everything.

Most Brainwashers will use their friends, stalk you during relationships, or exploit coincidence to show that they are aware of everything you do even in their absence.

## Perception Monopolization.

- The manipulator utters words that make you look deeper at yourself and start feeling vulnerable.

- The manipulator makes you unable to do things that are off-limits.

- The manipulator keeps you focused on them.

- The manipulator attempts to remove anything that they can't control from your life.

## Brainwashers attempt to weaken your ability to resist their control by doing the following:

- They keep you always busy meeting the very high standards they have set for cleanliness, parenting, and holiness.

- They look for tactics to make you feel guilty for refusing to accept their demands.

- They may claim that you have a sub-par character and insist that you change it.

- They may add other tasks to your life that are a lot more than the tasks expected in a normal relationship.

- They may demand that you attend social events that will help with improvement in their professional career and they may demand that you become friends with their boss's partner.

Can a person overcome brainwashing and heal from it? Yes, it is possible. If you are aware that you have been brainwashed, you can still heal from the effects and improve from what domestic violence has caused you and take back control of your mind. First, you need to learn how the manipulator put you under their control through the use of brainwashing techniques.

# Manipulating People

You will have times in your life when you don't get what you desire from people, but it doesn't mean you should be disappointed. Learn to manipulate the lemon salesperson when life gives you lemons. This is how to do it.

You need to understand that manipulating people can be generally a bad thing. You can learn how to do it and use it positively or use it to know when you are being manipulated in your daily interactions with people and protect yourself against the harm that manipulative people can cause.

## Become a master of your emotions.

Ideally, the person you are targeting won't have so much control over their emotions, but that shouldn't make you lazy. You need to be able to act since you are a master manipulator. You will need to master important skills that may include getting angry when it suits your needs or shedding a tear. Whether you are looking for sympathy, you want to incite fear, or anything else you want to do, it will depend on the particular situation you want to handle. So, mastering your own emotions is important to enable you to have the right tools for the task at hand.

## Logic and emotion.

Playing on people's emotions is the easiest way to manipulate them. If you give people enough time to think about something, they will likely make a logical decision. However, if you manipulate them into feeling a certain way that is of benefit to you, it will be easy for you to get what you want from them. This is known as emotional manipulation.

## Learn to flirt often and be charming.

You can't just throw tantrums or cry like children do whenever you need something. You have to be likable. Charm is needed when it comes to manipulating individuals. If you are an individual who is ridiculously likable a lot of the time, reacting with extreme emotion will greatly impact the situation. When you are able to control your emotions, it means you don't just have the ability to act, but you can keep your emotions in check most of the time. Although a charming personality is great, having the ability to flirt can also be helpful. The target generally feels poorly when manipulated, whether they are aware that they are being manipulated or not. The more the target likes you, the better things will flow. Disregard your own sexuality's boundaries and some suggestive touches can be thrown in when you believe that they will be effective. Lonely individuals and those with low self-esteem often find this tactic effective.

## Hide negative action in altruism.

Even if you are not a good person, you have to seem like you are. If there is ever a need to take a negative action like blaming someone else, whether it's the person's fault or yours, yelling at the target, or even criticizing behavior, you should do your best to wrap it in altruism. An altruist is not easily hated, so painting yourself as one is very effective. For instance, if your target didn't do what you wanted them to do and you yelled at them, you can frame the outburst as a way of helping the target. Apologize to them for the outburst and then tell them that you yelled at them because you felt they were not acting in their best interest. You can say that you care about them and have their best interest at heart and you are sorry you got so emotional. Tell the person it worries you to think that the person does not have their best interest at heart. On the other hand, you can remind a target when you are criticizing their behavior that you will always be there for them no matter what bad thing another individual does. Ensure that you always ask what you can do to help instead of just criticizing what other people do.

## Heal doubt and overcome trust issues.

Individuals who have been manipulated by people before find it hard to trust people and are often on the lookout for this type of behavior, so you have to open your eyes to check for signs. If you think that trust is a problem, the fastest way around that issue is to share a very private and personal thing with the target. It will be better if they feel you have enough trust in them to share something personal with them or if what you share is relevant to them. What is important is that they believe your story and not that it is true. Acting is also key.

When trying to manipulate another individual, the biggest enemy you will have is doubt. They might start getting to see that they are not behaving like themselves if they don't notice anything that is fishy about your behavior. Hopefully, you have learned about some of their problems at this point and found out what they desire to change in their lives. If the way they are acting is openly questioned by them, you need to let them know that change can be uncomfortable but it is necessary to make progress in their lives. Any negativity should be saved for a necessary emotional outburst. When you are trying to convince people to do what you desire, your best friend will always be positivity. The only time to use negative manipulation is when it is necessary as you can become an ineffective manipulator if there is too much negativity.

### Step to Take If You Are Discovered.

When many novice manipulators are discovered, they make the mistake of using the tactics discussed above. If your target starts calling you a manipulator, you should not respond with manipulative behavior. This is the worst thing you can do. Be a calm and normal person if you are caught. Allow them to assume control of the situation and don't even try to defend yourself. Once you have been caught, the best way to get out of the situation is to create doubt in your target's mind. Create doubt that is of benefit to you. If your target accuses you of being manipulative and you don't react like one who is manipulative, they will start doubting their thoughts and wonder if they assumed correctly or not. A lot of times, the target will already have an attachment to you and will embrace any excuse to believe they have made a wrong assumption about you. Oftentimes, when someone catches you, it is often because another manipulator or their friend has told them something about you. Be careful, be smart, and be prepared to surprise the person if you suddenly get discovered.

Do you have a friend who seems to follow this manual? Have people been targeting and manipulating you in the past?

# Avoiding Techniques Used in Brainwashing

Avoiding techniques used in brainwashing means that you have to avoid the brainwashers themselves, but you know that it can be hard to do this. For example, in advertising, you can't avoid brainwashers, and attempting to avoid them all can be expensive if you still like watching television and movies. The best thing to do is to cut out anything you can and, when it is difficult to cut out, seek balance. It is easy to find balance by simply giving yourself the information you need.

## You just need to do the following:

1. Pay attention to the manipulative message that you have received.

2. Look for a message that opposes the manipulative message, whether it is manipulative or not. Try to get the most unbiased and neutral account of that same message.

3. Compare the different sources you have and make a decision about how you feel.

Whether brainwashing is extreme or mild, isolation can make it possible. If the brainwashed message is what you keep hearing regularly, and you don't keep yourself open to alternatives, there is a high probability that you will accept what you hear and not think about it. If you want to avoid the brainwashing techniques we have discussed, you can surround yourself with more information instead of simply accepting the message that you feel comfortable with. After all, that is usually what the message aims to do.

## Techniques for Putting Ideas into People's Minds

Some people drive to their deaths in cars wired to bombs. An individual might be told to drive a car with a bomb nearer to a certain people or a place and then detonate it. While one individual may continue thinking about what they have been told and go on to drive the car to their death, another one may stop to think about it and eventually change their mind. Some members of a cult may be brainwashed into drinking poison by their leader. Cult members have committed many ritual suicides.

Brainwashing is powerful. It can convince people to do extreme things and even end their lives. There are many examples of people acting in stupid ways as a result of an idea that was put into their minds. From being convinced to kill innocent people to giving up all the worldly possessions they own, to joining a cult, it appears it is easier to brainwash the human mind than we often like to think.

There are also examples that are not extreme. If you have ever found yourself agreeing to do something you find unpleasant and don't want to do, if you have ever bought a product you didn't really want, or changed an opinion that you had about something after talking to somebody, you have experienced how other people can influence your mind. The mind is like a tablet that can be easily written upon and shaped by others. Have you always wondered what you can do to brainwash people?

Many people are fascinated with techniques to put ideas into the minds of individuals. Having the skill to enter into the dreams of people to learn their secrets could be something desirable. If there is any skill like this and you have it, you can enter someone's dream to plant an idea. The assumption is that an individual's mind can be changed from within, making them believe that the idea was their own idea.

You might be saying to yourself, "I can't enter people's dreams." You can still plant ideas in people's minds and get what you want without entering their dreams. These brainwashing techniques have the power to be destructive. Ensure that you use the techniques to brainwash individuals ethically and responsibly. Positive brainwashing has the power to make your relationships better and impress people at events.

What if you had the skills to plant ideas in the minds of people? Imagine what you could do with that. You might use it to get a date, a large sum of money, or a job. You could easily bring awkward disagreements to an end if you were able to plant an idea inside an individual's mind, while the individual believes that they actually thought of the idea themselves. So, how can you put an idea into a person's mind? We will discuss that.

## Embedded Commands and Word Ambiguity to Put Ideas into People's Minds

You might hear the sentence, "You must have made up your mind by now," and it may appear innocent until you discover that the command "by now" is contained in it. Salespeople and therapists often use this method of embedding commands in seemingly innocuous sentences.

Suppose you are trying to win over someone you like and want to date. "You love gadgets like me." This sentence contains "like me" which is the embedded command, and emphasizing certain words can have the effect of highlighting your message that is hidden, e.g. "I don't know what you want to do, but I will be going out, if you would like to go with me."

In essence, these techniques are reliant on clever wordplay. If you have ever misheard the lyrics of a song or fallen for a joke, you will know that there can be a misinterpretation of certain phrases. When you use ambiguity in your speech, you are subtly conveying a message without saying what you are saying directly. There are a variety of ambiguous sentences that you can use.

Hypnotists and practitioners of NLP usually change the way their patients think by pronouncing sentences in ambiguous ways. Look for any combination of words that you could put a hidden message into. The words should sound similar, and the hidden message can be in a seemingly innocent sentence. An innocent thing you say could bring another idea into the individual's mind.

## Priming.

Priming, which is often used by hypnotists is when an idea is suggested at the level that the other individual is not consciously aware of. If you provide a list of the words "rabbit," "chicken, and "dog," and ask a person to tell you one word that has the same rhyme as "hat," they will most likely say the word "cat" because they have a mind that is primed to think of animals.

Some people fool their participants into thinking that they telepathically guess which item their participants think of when they have primed their participants to think of a particular item.

Priming is also commonly used in advertising. Studies show that the amount of food people eat on a particular day can be increased with exposure to food advertisements. Marketing companies prime us to spend, and it is evident in all the images and messages we receive every day. When individuals are asked to recite the Ten Commandments before performing a task, the likelihood of cheating will be low, and when people are exposed to messages that have to do with old age, it can make people walk more slowly. Making an individual think along certain lines is capable of influencing the decisions the individual makes later.

Here is one trick you can try: prime the mind of your participant to think of red items. This can be done by pointing out a red thing, putting on a red shirt, or humming the tune to a song with red as the hook. You can do this creatively. Make sure that the tactics you use are not too obvious. Some minutes later, you can tell another friend involved in the conversation that you will be able to make a guess about what fruit your primed friend will mention. You can then ask your primed friend to mention the name of the first fruit that is on their mind. Because of the red priming, they will likely think and then say "apple".

Prime a person into being more agreeable by starting a conversation with questions that generate many "yes" responses. "It is a beautiful weather today, isn't it?" and some other questions that are yes-inducing can increase an individual's likelihood to say yes to suggestions you make.

If the idea you want to plant involves money, for instance, you want

to get an increase in salary, priming the person for kindness and empathy is better, as people are less inclined to share their wealth when they think about money. The most effective way to go about this is to make them think about their pride in their own generosity and their social connections by asking them about their hobbies or family.

## Brainwashing by Being Incomplete.

An individual might reject an idea if you offer it to them directly. Many people like to know that they are clever and that they thought of an idea on their own. We often reject ideas that other people offer us and cling to our own ideas. The trick here is to convince the individual that the idea you have is actually their own idea. This technique is common in sales and advertising. When an advert uses images of beautiful women wearing perfume, it does not mean that buying and using the perfume will make you look beautiful, but your brain has to put the pieces together.

If you want to plant an idea in a person's mind and make them believe the idea was actually their own idea, you can lay clues without making it obvious. You need to be patient when doing this because impatience will ruin everything. This doesn't need to be rushed, but it should be done over time.

If you and your partner are looking for holiday destinations and your partner prefers Europe for the holiday, while you have been dreaming of Hawaii, you could tell your partner about a crime that has happened in Europe and ensure that you talk about it occasionally or talk about how expensive things are there. You can then promote your preferred destination without making it too obvious.

One thing you can do is to play dumb. You can suggest to your partner that it would be nice if you could go somewhere that has great cocktails and beaches. If you effectively include things available in Hawaii in your suggestion without making it obvious, your partner might decide that Hawaii should be the place for the

holiday.

Once your partner starts thinking they are smart for bringing up the right destination, they will see it as their idea. They will form an attachment to the idea. You can also leave a beach picture lying around as this will create extra effect. This might not be consciously noticed by them, but the beach's picture will linger in their mind.

You can pretend that someone previously told you something. In this case, you can say something like, "I'm sure you are the one who told me..." or "You were saying that..." Even if the person can't remember saying this to you, a positive statement you attribute to them can make them claim it. Many individuals start believing they must have said it and then feel pride over the idea and claim ownership.

This method will be effective for giving advice. If a friend of yours finds it difficult to take advice, you may avoid giving them instructions and still tell them what to do. You can ask them leading questions. If you notice that they need to ask for an increase in salary at work, you could ask them if they have thought about what they need to do to make more money.

They will then think about a pay raise as the solution and you will smile and congratulate them on thinking about that idea. This technique is often used by therapists to make their clients feel in control of their lives. It gives their clients a feeling of power. This technique is effective as no one likes the feeling of being told what to do.

# Using Reverse Psychology

If you consider yourself someone who is a rebel, there is a probability that you don't like people telling you what to do. Instead of asking someone to tidy their room, and you tell them that you bet they couldn't keep their room clean even if they tried, don't you think they will be moved to tidy their room? People are wise these days and you can't just tell them the opposite of something you want them to do and expect them to do what you want. You can't just say, "Don't buy me a gift, then," when you actually want them to buy you a gift.

Reverse psychology is often used in advertising. If you have ever fallen in love with a product because it was limited or expensive, this technique might have been responsible for it. People don't often care much about what they can easily get; they seem to desire what is hard to get.

This is also used in dating. Once a woman has become attracted to you, you might say, "This would never work between us. I have to stop this now." You might also start acting as if you are not interested in a relationship with her. A woman who is used to always getting what she wants will start seeing you as a very interesting person and they will be convinced that you are the one they want to be with. Reverse psychology is considered more passive-aggressive than when an idea is planted into the mind.

Reverse psychology is usually more effective on argumentative or rebellious people. When you say something like, "The roller coaster is too scary; I don't think you would like it," it can make your friend get a ride ticket. They will want to try the ride because of your bold statement. Your friend will start wondering what you know about them and this can convince them to try the ride. Your friend will be thinking, "What do they know about me?" and this convinces your friend that trying the thing you suggested that they avoid was their own idea. Be careful when you use this technique. You don't use it for everything. For example, if you tell your friend not to date a girl, they might believe your words and stay single.

Although we are manipulated daily by politicians, advertisers, and others, the idea of manipulating someone's mind is ethically questionable. Manipulation from politicians might be in subtle form, where the politician says something that makes you feel good and you then conclude his other statements must also be good. Once

something is expensive, you might conclude that it must be good.

Brainwashing can be used to improve your life and it can also be used for evil. You can use it to make things flow smoothly for you without hurting anybody in the process. It can improve situations and make the world we live in a better place. Imagine using brainwashing to make more people care for the environment, to be kind to each other, or to eat more healthy meals. When you use techniques of brainwashing properly, it opens up doors that you may have considered impossible. If you don't want to use brainwashing techniques, you don't have to.

## How to Avoid Manipulation

### Accept thoughts, fears, and pain.
You will experience unpleasant feelings as you heal from brainwashing. You need to deprogram your mind and get out of your manipulator's world. When you accept the manipulator's plans and how they mask themselves with a nice face to try to harm you, you will experience one of the most rational and irrational emotions, which is fear. A therapist or good domestic attorney for violence can help you overcome your fears in a productive and healthy manner.

### Gain knowledge about different kinds of abuse.
There is power in knowledge, and you can use it to successfully stop your manipulator's attempts to degrade and humiliate you. The

probability of feeling worse about the words and actions of your manipulator will be low when you know your abuser harms you because they want to control you. Learn and understand as much as possible what you need to know about domestic violence and abuse. With time, you will know how to recognize the kinds of verbal abuse your partner makes you experience. When you understand the different types of abuse and you can identify them, you will be able to detach from harmful words and behaviors as you will know when your manipulator is trying to cause you harm. Be aware of what type of abuse is out there, and how the abuse looks and sounds, and note the feelings the abuse gives you. One question you might have asked yourself is why does the abuser abuse you? Do not spend too much time trying to research the answer.

## Put an end to isolation.

One fast way to get over any fear that you have is opening up about your feelings and the situation. It is wise to discuss the manipulation with a therapist. You may not be ready to talk about this, but you can start by talking about last night's football match or talking about the weather, as you will gain some confidence with this. When you isolate yourself, it doesn't completely make brainwashing end. Surround yourself with individuals who are aware of your abuse and who can give you their support.

## Dealing with fear and anxiety.

Leaving the manipulator is an appropriate stress reliever for individuals who have experienced manipulation. That way, the victim will experience peace in a way that they have never imagined they would experience. Many individuals are not ready to quit, and they may choose to remain with the manipulator forever. You can handle stress and anxiety by having proper nutrition, practicing hypnosis if you are a victim of abuse, getting proper medical care, listening to music, practicing meditation techniques, practicing breathing techniques, and taking a walk during your spare time.

# Manipulation and Force

At least, psychological and social force is incorporated in every case of manipulation; it doesn't involve physical force. You also need to know that there is a difference between brainwashing and manipulation. In brainwashing, the individual is aware that the aggressor is an enemy. During wars, the belief system of prisoners was changed through the use of brainwashing. Physical force is involved in brainwashing, and the individual concerned is made to do what they would normally not do. However, the brainwashing effects disappear when they escape the enemy.

This aspect increases mind manipulation's effectiveness and makes it more dangerous than abuse, torture, physical coercion, and brainwashing. Remember that physical coercion is not involved in mind manipulation, but it has a higher effectiveness than other techniques. Although brainwashing can change an individual's behavior, mind manipulation can change the person's entire beliefs, thinking processes, attitudes, behaviors, and personality. Also, the individual will happily and actively take part in the change process, because they believe that it is the best thing to do.

It is difficult to believe that you were actually being manipulated by someone you liked, trusted, and helped. That is something that makes it difficult to help an individual in a manipulative relationship. They find it hard to believe that they are being manipulated by the manipulator. The victim will find it hard to let go of the changes that had taken place even when they are free from the manipulator's grip. When we are pushed to make decisions, the effect doesn't last as long as when we make decisions for ourselves. It is difficult to admit that an individual who is close to us was responsible for certain decisions we made.

Ensure that you don't harm other people or ignore their desires even though you have learned how to use manipulation to achieve your desires. Manipulation will involve persuasion, coaxing, charm, and maybe some trickery and misdirection. You shouldn't be using manipulation to make everyone give you what you desire regardless of the negative consequences that may be involved. Manipulation should be done in such a way that you get what you want and also leave the other individual better than you met them.

Your desires are not the only important issues, so you need to use manipulation in such a way that you do not hurt other people. Understand that those around you have needs that might match with your needs and you can find a situation that is a win for all involved. People will easily trust you if they feel that their needs matter and they don't feel manipulated.

# CHAPTER SIX:
## Dark Psychology Red Flags

There are red flags of dark psychology that you need to know about. This is necessary to understand it fully. Once you have this knowledge, you can use it when you want and you can also protect yourself from the manipulation and influence of others.

## Let us take a look at some common dark psychology red flags:

### Isolate victims from family and friends.

People using dark psychology on others may try to isolate the individuals from their family and friends to be able to exert more control over them and influence their actions.

### Acting too nice, shallow flattery, and superficial compliments.

The most charming and nicest girl or guy in the room is usually looked at suspiciously by therapists. This is often the case because they are usually putting on a show and on the high side of acceptable narcissism. They are hiding their true personality and not showing it. You need to be careful because they may do it in a humble way which makes it hard to notice or they may do it in a flashy attention-seeking manner. If a person is always flattering you, giving you compliments, and being so sweet and nice to you, that person is probably too good to be true. When people want to hook you in and then manipulate you and disappoint you later, they usually display this behavior. At the beginning of a relationship, if a person behaves more like your butler than actually acting like your girlfriend or boyfriend that they are, this person may have attachment or boundary issues. Look for nice romantic partners and friends but if it appears phony, over the top, or not genuine, then you need to pay attention.

## Pressure people to make fast decisions.

People using dark psychology on others may try to pressure these individuals into making fast decisions, thereby giving the individuals little or no time to reflect on the request and consider it.

## Intimidation tactics.

People controlling others through dark psychology may use intimidation tactics to control their victims and influence their behavior.

## Making victims feel ashamed or guilty.

People may use dark psychology to try to manipulate individuals by making them feel ashamed or guilty.

## Flatter people excessively.

People who use dark psychology may gain other people's trust and influence over them by flattering them excessively. Flattery exploits people's healthy and normal need to build authentic connections with other people. Social interactions may use flattery as a tactic in which the flatterer desires to gain something from the person they are flattering. This tactic of coercion is quite effective. When someone flatters you, they make you feel better about yourself, which makes you start seeing them in a more positive way. This increases the likelihood of you complying with the plan they have for you. Potential voters may be flattered by politicians. Employees may be flattered by their employers to give them an artificial morale boost and increase their productivity. Clergy might get tithes from their congregation by flattering them. When a leader is criticized, they might use flattery to disarm their critics and shame them. A sexual predator might groom a person they are targeting by using flattery.

The flattery is usually directed at something that the recipient considers important to them and it is done in a way that doesn't appear obvious enough for it to be confronted or pointed out.

## How Flattery Manipulates an Individual's Emotions

Flattery is capable of creating a false sense of admiration and trust, which can make an individual more open to other forms of manipulation. It has the ability to make a person feel important and special, which can lower the person's defenses and make them more open to the requests of the manipulator.

Flattery has the ability to manipulate people's emotions, thereby clouding their judgment and making them feel good about themselves. This can make it hard for a person to see the true motives of the manipulator and recognize that the manipulator is manipulating them. A sense of loyalty or obligation is created, and this can make a person feel like they need to do what the manipulator is asking them to do in order for the manipulator to maintain the positive opinion they have about them or in order that they will not let the manipulator down.

The manipulator can also use flattery to distract their target from their true intentions, making the target look away from their actions' negative consequences and focus on the positive feedback they are getting. This makes the target depend on the approval and validation of the manipulator, making the target rely more on them and then do whatever they ask them to do.

## Combination of Manipulation and Flattery

Flattery may appear appealing and enjoyable at first, just like a sweet candy. But too much of it can be harmful to you.

In the same way that consuming too much candy can cause tooth decay and weight gain, too much flattery can make an individual lack critical thinking and have a distorted sense of reality.

Just like candy is meant to be enjoyed in moderation, ensure that you are wary of too much flattery and be aware that it can deceive and manipulate people. Manipulation can be likened to when the strings of the puppet are being pulled by the puppet master. Being in control, the puppet master, who is the manipulator, has the ability to make the victim do whatever they want them to do, but the victim has no idea that they are being manipulated and may think that their decisions are being made by them.

Manipulation involves influencing or controlling an individual in a deceptive way, causing them to do things that they may not have considered doing if they were not manipulated. In the same way that a puppet does not know anything about the manipulation, an individual being manipulated may have no idea of the manipulator's true motives. But when flattery is combined with manipulation, it is a dangerous mix because when they are combined, they work well at controlling and influencing people. The individual may not even know that the manipulator is manipulating them, and this is what makes this type of manipulation harmful.

The individual may be doing whatever the manipulator asks them to do out of loyalty and love because they think that the manipulator actually has their best interests at heart.

This makes it hard for the individual to recognize what is happening and resist the manipulation, and the individual may end up doing things that are harmful to them and not in their own best interest.

## Flattery can be used to manipulate people in the following contexts:

**A salesperson's flattery:** A salesman or woman can use flattery to make you buy a product you don't need.

**Flattering a partner in a relationship:** When a partner constantly dishes compliments to the other partner, they may be doing their best to manipulate or control them.

**Flattery from family members:** A family member may be trying to manipulate you into doing something that is in their own interest by constantly giving you compliments.

**Flattery from friends:** If you have a friend who always compliments you, they may be trying to get you to do something that is in their own interest that you don't want to do.

**Flattery on social media:** A social media user may use flattery to get close to you. They may constantly comment on your posts or like your posts because they are trying to gain your trust or attention.

**Flattering colleagues at work:** You may have a boss who always praises you at work. This person may be praising you because they want you to do something that will benefit them and not you.

**Flattery in dating:** An individual may try to win your affection by using flattery to manipulate you into going deeper into the relationship than you would like.

Flattery deceives an individual while praise offers encouragement. When someone flatters another person, they hope to get something done without thinking about the individual who receives the flattery. The flatterer usually has an ulterior motive that is beneficial to them alone. Praise, on the other hand, is beneficial to the person receiving it as it encourages the person being praised to see the positive aspects of life. Praise makes it possible for others to recognize the talents they have, increase their self-esteem, give direction, and restore hope. It is helpful to both the receiver and the giver.

# CHAPTER SEVEN:
## Dark Psychology in Relationships

An individual in a relationship can fulfill their own needs by using the techniques of dark psychology at the expense of their partner.

Can you make someone open up and connect deeply with them? To answer this question easily, you need to think back to how often and when somebody said any of the following to you, "you are the only person I can really discuss this issue with," "You are the only person who truly understands what I am talking about," "you are the first individual I have ever talked to about this." If people usually say this kind of stuff to you regularly, it means you definitely know how to get other people to open up to you and you know how to connect with them on a deeper level. The answers show that somebody found you to be a confidant. You are a person they can trust and be open, honest, and vulnerable with.

If you have heard these sentences several times in your life from people who are close to you and even strangers you are just getting to know, it means that you have the ability to connect with people easily and on a deeper level. You may be thinking that your connection with people is just a mere coincidence and you just happened to be in the right place at the right time. The lifeblood of all relationships that are important is your ability to connect deeply with other individuals. If you examine your connections and relations to see how they started, you can make a conscious effort to increase the level of your interactions. Examining your connections and relationships will reveal to you that most individuals have "shadow" parts that they hide and only reveal to a few individuals. You can make a true connection with someone if you can find your way to these shadow parts they have, and you can do this by accepting the person for who they really are. When you analyze the most vulnerable moments that you have shared with others, you will discover that these moments of opening up, vulnerability, and connection did not just happen by random coincidence.

## Making A Person Fall in Love with You

Have you ever been drawn to an individual whose presence brings you warmth and also sudden coldness? The person comes close to you and then retreats, and this pattern leaves you wanting more of them. This relationship is not just a troubled one; the person is deliberate with this tactic. This dark manipulation technique switches between pleasure and pain.

The person lures you in with affection and then comes the sting of their absence. Isn't this confusing? One day, you are showered with so much attention, and the next day, you are left alone in the cold, wondering if you are even worth anything to that person. This dark manipulation technique thrives on this kind of confusion. The cycle continues. There is a period where affection is intense and then after that comes a sudden withdrawal of affection, where the warmth disappears. You become addicted to this push-and-pull game where you don't know what the rules are and your emotional well-being is at risk.

Everyone is a manipulator, at least to an extent. Connections are fostered through the use of social cues like eye contact and smiles. But when someone is using manipulation to control someone to their own advantage and not to form a connection, a line is crossed. This is not a healthy interaction. The strategy is used to make a person dependent on the manipulator to give them emotional validation.

There is a price associated with a manipulated heart. Such manipulation has a steep cost. The manipulated person usually experiences a plummeting self-esteem, and they also experience depression and anxiety. There is a relentless pursuit of approval, which binds the person tighter to the manipulator, who is the source of the person's pain. This dependency is harmful, and the cycle feeds on the victim's need for validation.

Let us discuss some dark psychological tactics that you can use to make someone fall in love with you.

Select the victim that is suitable, you need to choose the suitable person because you can't pick someone who has high self-esteem and is happy with their life. The person has to have a need in their life that has not been met. To get the person to fall in love with you, you need to find their place of vulnerability and then provide validation for the person's vulnerability.

Send the person mixed signals to make them believe that they have your heart and then withdraw from them. The person has to feel the loss of losing you and you have to make that happen.

You need to have qualities that are contrasting. For instance, if there is a woman you like and want to make her fall in love with you, having an air of femininity to strike a balance is important. A person who is too masculine shows insecurity because over-masculinity shows over-compensation. When you strike a balance, you appear more trustworthy.

Talk about other women as this will help you create a triangle of desire. The female you talk about should have a look that is opposite to how she looks. When you let her know the type of women you find attractive, it creates competition. This can inflict pain, and you don't have to be afraid of doing this. You have the power to also inflict pleasure if you can inflict pain.

Plant insecurities in her and do it at a subconscious level. You can do this by talking about something you are aware will be difficult for her to meet, mentioning it while having a conversation with her, and then changing the topic quickly. Don't give her time to elaborate on the topic you mentioned. You just need to plant the seed in the woman's subconscious mind.

Set up barriers and challenges. Interaction becomes a lot better when you set intentional challenges. Create temptation that will bring the relationship to life and enjoy teasing her. Women usually appreciate men who tease them. They will feel frustrated, and this frustration increases their desire for you.

Giving the woman thoughtful gifts helps. Pay attention to them and find out what they love. You can then give them a unique gift. When you give them gifts, it makes them believe that they are on your mind. During the relationship, you can take a step back and then return.

Disarm the woman with vulnerability. When you show vulnerability, the woman is able to see the real human in you.

Be unable to control yourself when you are around her, showing her that you find it hard to resist her charm and she is too beautiful. People enjoy being admired by others so this could be a flattering situation for them. It also helps you to hide these tactics.

Give the woman space because she will fall in love with you when you are not around her. When you back off a bit, it allows her to think of you, and her view of you is also enhanced.

Engage in the woman's deepest narcissism. If you embody the idealized person that she is, she will love you. Don't give her room to take you for granted. Ensure that you use pleasure, pain, and absence as it will make her appreciate you.

Find the woman's secret fantasy and make it a reality. If you can do this, you will see that she will become obsessed with you. She experiences your power and also experiences you when she feels your boundaries, so ensure that she feels your boundaries.

The more subtle your mixed signals and your disinterest the better things will work. You have to make the woman not know you, but make her interpret you.

# Techniques of Dark Psychology in Dating

## 1. Wearing a mask.

This dark psychology technique is when someone wears a mask of the ideal partner, thereby pretending to have the same goals and interests as a person with the aim of advancing the relationship. For instance, a person might pretend to share similar interests and hobbies with you or love those hobbies and interests when they actually don't like them.

**Strategy for avoidance:** Maintain your interests and individuality in a relationship. If an individual appears to be too eager to align with your preferences, ensure that you are cautious about that. Create room for open discussions about differences as this will contribute to establish a genuine connection.

## 2. Pretending to have low interest.

Female dark psychologists stay in control of their relationship by pretending to have low interest in their partner. This makes them appear as a prize, thereby manipulating the man to continue chasing them. The lady might pretend that she is not interested in the relationship when she is really interested.

**Strategy for avoidance:** Understand the value of interest and mutual respect in a relationship. Avoid chasing an individual who keeps playing hard to get. There has to be equal investment from both parties to have a healthy relationship.

## 3. False commitment.

A man may use dark psychology to deceive a lady by pretending that they are interested in having a committed relationship while lying to them and giving them false promises. The man might make the lady believe that he wants to have a future with her but avoid making an actual commitment to the relationship.

**Strategy for avoidance:** An individual should ensure that they make honest and open communication a priority in their relationship. They should see that actions and words align over time. They should also pay attention and notice any discrepancies that may occur between a person's actual behavior and their stated intentions. Expectations and long-term goals should be discussed early in the relationship.

## 4. Using sex as a reward or punishment.
Some people use sex as a punishment or reward to achieve what they want in their relationship. For example, they might control their partner by withholding intimacy from them.

**Strategy for avoidance:** Ensure that intimacy is not used as a bargaining chip in a relationship. Intimacy should be based on consent and mutual desire. Be open about communication and talk about boundaries and expectations concerning physical intimacy.

# CHAPTER EIGHT:
## Dark Psychology in Business and Groups

Dark psychology is capable of manipulating employees in the workplace into ignoring their own interests and prioritizing the interests of the company.

## Techniques of Dark Psychology in Business

### 1. Dark leadership personality traits.

Some organizations are good at unintentionally encouraging dark personality traits in the organization's managers, thereby making the work environment toxic. When choosing employers, employees need to be cautious and avoid depending on superiors for support. For example, a company's manager might manipulate the workers into doing more work without adequate compensation for the extra time worked by putting emphasis on how important it is for the company to be successful.

**Strategy of avoidance:** Check for the leadership qualities that potential managers possess when you are choosing an employer. Stay away from organizations that promote toxic work environments. Be an advocate for proper compensation and fair treatment in your place of work.

### 2. Corporate manipulation.

A company may guilt-trip employees into accepting unfavorable conditions for the company's greater good. Slogans such as "we are a family" and "employees matter," are used by companies to guilt-trip employees and make them care more about the company's benefit than their personal well-being.

**Strategy for avoidance:** Pay attention to corporate messages and slogans that promote sacrificing oneself for the organization. Make your rights as an employee and your well-being a priority. Seek fairness and transparency in the organization's policies.

The impact of dark psychology is undeniably far-reaching and profound even though it may not hold an official designation in the realm of psychology. This discipline involves using psychological tactics to accomplish sinister ends. When you understand these techniques, you will be able to recognize when you are being manipulated and then protect yourself from the effects. Staying vigilant and informed in the face of potential manipulation is important.

# Understanding Sales Psychology

Salespeople use sales psychology to make their prospective customers feel good about themselves. People remember more the feelings you made them experience than what you say to them. This means that customers remember more of how you make them feel. Therefore, tactics that are very powerful in sales are the ones that make customers feel really good about themselves, and these tactics include psychological ones. Sales psychology has the ability to make prospects feel good about themselves. It helps salesmen and saleswomen close deals.

Things go deeper than simply feeling good, even though it is at the core of sales psychology. Why salespeople use psychological tactics explains how they use the tactics in their sales strategy.

# Using Psychology in Sales

When psychology in sales is involved, the reason salespeople use it explains how they use it. Making customers feel really good about themselves is at the core of why successful salesmen and saleswomen use psychology.

But, you don't really get the whole story from that, as you could also make someone feel good in many other ways. Sales reps sometimes feel like they are being manipulative or malicious by using sales psychology. Because prospects have a short attention span and many of them would get lost during the sales process, sales reps use psychology. It is not just prospects that have a short attention span; humans in general do. This is why sales psychology is used.

If they didn't use sales psychology, it would be hard to get prospects to focus and not get lost during the sales process. If they don't use psychology, prospects would not focus on the solution in front of them and would struggle to make the right decision that would help them.

Let us look at the how. Salespeople use psychology to convince prospects to make a particular decision. With sales psychology, the salespeople tap into the brains of their prospects to influence their decisions. If you are a salesperson, don't ever feel bad about swaying prospect decision-making by using psychological tactics. All you are doing is to help them see that you have the right solution for them, and this makes them feel amazing.

A difference exists between low-pressure selling and high-pressure selling. Most people do not enjoy feeling like someone is selling something to them. For instance, do you enjoy getting the sense that the salesperson doesn't care a bit about you and is only selling to you in their own interest? Most people dislike being sold to.

Part of high-pressure selling is the feeling that you are being sold to. It involves the feeling that someone is making you make a decision to buy. And this experience is not a positive sales experience. Low-pressure selling is the opposite kind of approach. Prospects feel good with the psychological tactics it uses, and when prospects feel good, more deals are closed.

Moreover, these tactics are within the approach of low-pressure selling. People who are the best at sales do their best to make their prospects feel good. They do this because they know that someone is empowered and they are close to closing a deal when the customer feels good.

When sales psychology tactics are used in a low-pressure sales approach, it leads to a win for salespeople and prospects.

## 1. Techniques of sales psychology used for lead generation.

There is probably nothing better in sales than when leads come to you, instead of creating the list yourself. Lead generation, which is the first stage of the sales process, can be started with sales psychology.

You can begin to fill your sales funnel with leads by allowing them to come to you. Before you even reach out, you can even warm them up to the person that you are.

These two sales tactics knock lead generation out of the park by using psychology.

### Mirror the identity of your lead.

People naturally gravitate towards those people who they feel are like them. Most especially, individuals who they believe think like them, act like them or have the same values as them.

Although it is a little unnerving to realize that people unconsciously gravitate towards what they consider similar, this fact can be used to your advantage in sales.

Work with your marketing team to release content that reflects some aspect of your ideal lead.

For instance, if you have ideal leads with a social media profile that shows how committed they are, you can do the same thing in your own content. It doesn't mean that you should do a full sustainability campaign, but you can even make a few posts that will do the trick if it shows your similarity.

This will then make your lead recognize that you and them are

similar, and it will make them more likely to reach out. And even if you are the one who makes the first move, the likelihood of them responding will increase.

## Show potential leads your social proof.

I'm sure you know what peer pressure is. It doesn't suddenly end after high school. You can get leads into the sales funnel by using a modified version of peer pressure, and this is a sales psychology tactic that is very effective. This is called "pressure" in life and called "social proof" in sales.

Social proof allows potential leads to see that others are taking advantage of the solution your business is providing and they are reaping the benefits.

For instance, you can make a post on your social media platforms talking about how the lives of your current customers have become better after working with you. This will make your potential leads believe that it will work for them if it actually works for those people. And then a new lead will enter your sales funnel. Although some people think that social proof is a manipulative, misleading, and negative tactic, this is not the case.

If you believe you have a solution that is excellent and has the ability to solve the challenges that people have, what is preventing you from getting the solution into their hands?

There is no harm if you need to use social proof to make leads see that you can solve their problems.

## 2. Techniques of sales psychology for outreach.

After filling your pipeline with leads, you can reach out to them directly and turn them into prospects.

Whether this is the first time you are connecting with them, or they showed interest in you themselves, sales psychology can be used by you to your advantage.

Salespeople can use the following two psychological techniques during the sales process' outreach stage.

## Expectations should be uprooted.

Are you aware that your brain is constantly trying to work ahead of you? Are you aware that it tries to predict what is about to come next in a sequence and you don't even know it?

Your brain will be a bit taken aback when it sees something other than what it wanted to see in a particular sentence.

This think-ahead strategy of the brain can be used by sales reps to their advantage. You can do it this way:

Try to flip your language when you are writing a sales cold email. Instead of saying what the prospect would expect you to say, uproot what they expect you to say. When the expectations of the brain are uprooted, the brain remembers it for a long time. Uprooting expectations helps you stay memorable. When you are memorable, it is also a sales psychology tactic. The prospect will see you as an authority in their domain when you are memorable.

## Reciprocity.

Imagine this scenario: You have the perfect cold-calling script as well as your ideal leads. You manage to put in some sentences after the lead answers the phone. But the line then goes dead all of a sudden.

What is the best way to cold-call leads and get them to listen and not hang up the phone? Sales psychology can do the trick.

If you are making cold calls to your prospects and taking some of their time, you should have a valuable thing to give them in return.

For instance, you can inform the prospect that you ran an analysis on their company and you discovered a problem that you want to discuss with them. You are offering them value when you do this. Reciprocity is then initiated.

The reciprocity concept entails that someone will naturally want to give you something in return when you give them something valuable. So, if you show the prospects something valuable or hidden about their company that they are not aware of, the prospects will set up a formal sales meeting to reciprocate your generosity.

Remember, don't wish to get something for nothing. You need to offer the prospects something that they will consider valuable when you cold call to make them reciprocate the favor.

## 3. Techniques of sales psychology for qualifying.

At this point, you have reached out to leads and made them agree to a sales call. Great. As you qualify these leads as a fit for your solution, ensure that you keep the psychological momentum going. Keep in mind that this stage's goal is to find out the pain points of the prospects and then begin to build rapport. Successful salesmen and saleswomen use these psychological tactics to do both of those things:

### The fear of missing out.

The fear of missing out or FOMO is a term that has been made popular by social media. It is a feeling that people get when they think that they will lose out on a positive thing if they fail to purchase a particular product or service.

For instance, a company selling sales services can make you feel that you are missing out when you don't buy from them, and they can use tactics to make you feel this way. So, you will want to buy from them because you believe you will have a perfectly organized sales process.

It is not too early to start creating a sense of FOMO even though you are still in the process of qualifying the prospect. A highly effective tactic is sharing a case study as it will make the prospects feel some fear of missing out.

You can share a case study with them when you get to the end of

your initial sales call, as it will help to create a sense of FOMO inside the prospects. This will increase their readiness to move ahead into the sales process' next stage.

## Make the prospects feel in control.

You need to ask the prospects the right questions if you want to know their pain points.

However, when you ask questions, it creates a negative side effect where the prospect feels like they have no control at all over the situation. This can make them leave.

What if you can get the information you need from the prospects without asking them questions? The good news is, you can. These negotiation tactics can make the prospect talk about their problems and you don't have to ask them any questions before they talk about the problems. The effect is the same as questioning. This way, they feel like they are in control of the situation and you also get the information you need.

Prospects' self-esteem increases when you make them feel in control. They will not feel trampled by you but will feel empowered by you.

## 4. Techniques of sales psychology for the sales pitch.

Lastly, you are at the sales pitch. Unless you have a sales cycle that is very drawn out, this is the final step before the buying decision is made.

You can use the pitch as the time to shine. If you still feel like you haven't convinced the prospect enough, this is the time to let them see all the value your solution will bring them. When you are making sales pitches, you can use sales psychology to show the prospects that you are capable of turning all the issues they have into strengths.

## Dress and look the part.

Although this one is quite obvious, don't forget to dress as the

individual you want to be when you show up to your sales pitches. And this person, hopefully, is a salesperson that is successful. Ensure that you show up as if you are a successful salesperson even if you don't believe in yourself at the moment.

When you dress the part of a salesperson that is successful, an additional layer of storytelling is added to your pitch. You also feel like you are at your very best. This will help you emit positive energy when you feel great about yourself, and your prospects will also feel a positive energy. The prospects embrace your pitch even more when they feel the positive energy.

Dressing the part makes you feel good about yourself, and the aura of the sales pitch is changed for the better.

## Use the customer's needs to create a storyline.

What makes individuals purchase the things that they purchase?

People usually purchase products or services that match their internal narrative. A narrative can be referred to as a story.

Stories help with sales, and it is left for you to create a story out of your prospect's problems when making the sales pitch. While your prospects should be the superhero in the story, your solution should be what magically saves the day.

Prospects' emotional desires are satisfied by stories. And this is responsible for their purchasing decision. You should be thinking big if you desire to create a storyline that is effective. If you want to make your pitches into a story that your prospects will find hard to resist, here is how to do it. Although this might sound crazy in the beginning, your sales will sink if you fail to create a storyline that is effective.

## 5. Techniques of sales psychology for closing the deal.

Although the sales pitch might seem like the process has come to an end, you might still lose the sale when you try to lay the deal on the table. This stage of closing the deal is usually the most difficult. But, you can still change things. Using the following sales psychology tactics at the end of the process will help you stay in control of the situation until the end.

## Reduce the number of available options.

Have you ever walked into an ice cream store, only to find many flavors that blew you away? The store has every kind of flavor, including even the ones you have never seen.

You suddenly discover that you have been at the counter for more than ten minutes without making a decision. You are not the only one getting frustrated, but those standing behind you are also getting frustrated.

Although your business may not be an ice cream store, your prospects can also experience something similar if the options you give them are too many. It will overwhelm them and they will not have a good experience.

Whether you believe this or not, the likelihood of abandoning a situation or having a negative experience increases when you have more options. So, ensure that you don't confuse your prospects with too many options to select from when you lay your deal down on the table. Giving them about 3 options is okay. You are not helping them by giving them more options, but the opposite is actually the case. You can give them 3 choices so they don't begin to develop negative feelings right before you close the sale.

## Create time that is limited.

So, you have laid your offer on the table, but your prospects are not forthcoming, but they are hesitating. A long silence starts to fill the room. Your prospects are not screaming yes to your offer as you thought they would. Instead, they are contemplating what decision to take. Although you have done your best right up until this point, you are beginning to feel that you are losing the sale.

To stop this from happening to you, ensure that you create a sense of

urgency when you discuss the deal's terms. Creating a sense of urgency means that you should make your prospects feel like they will lose out on something valuable if they delay accepting your offer.

An effective way to do this is to give them a unique offer, in which you include something extra in their deal if they are willing to accept the offer right away.

When you offer your prospects a special thing for only a limited time, it will make them quickly say yes to the deal.

You need to know how to work with people if you want to be successful in business. It will be difficult for you to be successful in sales if you can't work well with people.

# Dark Psychology in Groups

Dark psychology is used in group settings, where the group leaders aim to increase their influence and control over the members of the group. Let us take a look at some examples of how the techniques of dark psychology can manifest in groups:

### 1. Fabricating an external threat.
A leader of a group may try to unify the group by fabricating a common external threat. This will create cohesion among the group members and also create a sense of protection. The group leader might make an imaginary enemy that the group can only defeat.

**Strategy for avoidance:** Pay attention to attempts to create an external enemy and be critical of it. Check whether the perceived threat is actually exaggerated to manipulate people or if it is real.

Encourage unity and cooperation based on shared values and not threats that were manufactured.

## 2. Dismissing dissenting opinions.

Group leaders may dismiss or discredit dissenting opinions that

abound within the group, thereby ensuring the group members stay loyal to the beliefs and commands of the group. This may include labeling dissenters as outsiders or traitors.

**Strategy for avoidance:** Create room for an inclusive and open environment where you embrace diverse opinions. Pay attention to groups that stop dissenting voices because it can result in groupthink. Encourage constructive criticism and healthy debate.

## 3. Exaggerating the severity of problems.

Leaders of groups often exaggerate the severity of issues, thereby convincing the group members that it will be difficult to solve the problems on their own and that they need the guidance of the group to solve the issues. This then increases the group members' dependency on the group leader. For example, the leader of a cult might inflate the perceived threats that their followers are receiving to their well-being.

**Strategy of avoidance:** Ensure that you pay attention and ask questions when you find yourself facing exaggerated problems. Look at different perspectives and verify them independently before accepting an issue's severity. Avoid making hasty decisions borne from inflated concerns.

# CONCLUSION

After reading this book, understanding people's thoughts and how to change them will no longer be a problem for you. We have talked about how you can use dark psychology to do this.

Dark psychology is a common technique many individuals and companies use to influence lives daily. Politicians use it to convince people and get what they want from them. Salespeople use it to control people's minds and get them to make the decision to buy.

It is important that you understand your emotions and those of others, as it will help you read their minds. Practice listening with empathy when someone is talking to you, and ensure that you stay open and calm.

Flattery can be combined with manipulation. However, the combination of flattery and manipulation is very powerful and works well at controlling and influencing people. The individual being manipulated may not even know they are being manipulated, making this type of manipulation harmful.

The person being manipulated may be doing everything the manipulator asked them to do out of loyalty and love, thinking that the manipulator has their best interests at heart. They do not know that the manipulator is manipulating them for their own advantage and don't have their interests at heart.

Now that you are aware of this, you will know when you are being manipulated and when to use the techniques to your advantage. Remember to use the methods we have discussed for good and not to harm anyone.

If you are in a situation where you need to understand what someone is thinking to know the right words to say to them, the techniques in this book will guide you. You have been dreaming of traveling to a particular country for a holiday, but your partner prefers another destination; you can put ideas into your partner's mind, and they will think the idea of traveling to your dream destination is actually their own idea. Also, if you are trying to get a crush to like you and you are not sure if they will say yes to your friendship offer, you can study their body language and come up with the right words.

Reverse psychology can help you in dating. You might act as if you are not interested in having a relationship with a woman when you really like her. This will make the woman start seeing you as a very interesting person and make up her mind that she wants to be with you.

You can use the techniques we have discussed in this book in different situations. As you continue to practice the methods, you will get better and become a master at using dark psychology to understand people's thoughts in no time.

# The Mind Games THEY Play

11 Proven Strategies to Identify, Understand, and Resist Manipulation and Master the Art of Human Psychology.

## HALBERT WARD

# INTRODUCTION

Reading a person's mind is a skill that anybody can learn. Anybody can play mind games. You can know what your client needs even before they open their mouth to say anything or you can know the best way to approach your boss to get a favorable outcome. When you develop an intuition about the things that others find valuable, it will help you move further in life.

Perceptive people often enjoy more success in their personal lives and professional lives. Individuals who perform excellently well are not always the smartest individuals; they are the individuals who form a good connection with other people and possess a higher emotional quotient.

People are always sending signals about what they are thinking about. Although they are sending these signals all the time, practice is required to tune in. When the messages you are getting from an individual are saying that you and the individual are not on the same page, the clues you are getting are telling you to take a step back and then redirect. They are saying you should change the conversation to something else or change the way you are approaching the conversation. There are a variety of ways you can read people's minds or guess what is on their minds and then develop better personal and business relationships.

In this book, we discuss the interesting world of mind control and equip you with the necessary tools and strategies you need to develop healthy relationships with people and protect yourself from manipulation.

So, what is mind control, and how can you control a person's mind?

The subject of mind control is a captivating and even concerning one that people have been curious about for ages. Whether you want to understand what is actually happening in toxic relationships or you want to explore the manipulative tactics that leaders of cults usually use, learning about mind control is important for your emotional and mental well-being.

When you understand mind control's principles, you get better equipped to recognize when you are being manipulated and you are able to resist its influence. Having this knowledge empowers you and makes you able to make informed decisions that will help you in your life, develop healthy relationships that are based on respect and trust, and you are able to assert your boundaries.

The purpose of this book is to help you understand how mind control works so that you can use it to improve your life and protect yourself from manipulators who want to use it against you. The book is not about teaching you how to control the minds of people for unethical purposes.

We will discuss the factors that are responsible for manipulation, symptoms to look out for, and practical strategies you can use to break free from the manipulator's grip. You will learn to form healthy relationship dynamics and your dating experiences will be enhanced.

The process of getting a person to change their mind involves taking into account the person's beliefs, life experience, education, and values. This will help you know the right approach to take. Since everything is reliant upon the willingness of the individual to accept an idea that is new, continuously providing more and more data because you want to back up your claim might cause them to resist all evidence and discard it. Therefore, instead of making them feel intimidated, you can make them feel comfortable as it will open them to suggestions.

You might attempt to change a person's core values. It is often impossible to prove an individual's belief system wrong. However, you can make them experience reality differently, and this can make them change the core beliefs that they have. When a person witnesses a moment like this without any external influence, there is a belief by the subject that they are questioning reality objectively. The influence this has on them is stronger than if a person told them to question an idea coming from someone else.

Making an individual change their mind and do what you want them to do does not have to be complicated. If you master the art of human psychology, you can use it to influence individuals by making the right appeals that they will comply with. You can change the minds of people by following steps that work subconsciously on them.

Is there any individual that you have struggled to persuade previously? After reading this book, you will be able to easily persuade them. You will develop the skills needed to face less resistance to your ideas and people will be more receptive to changing their minds.

This book will give you deeper insights on manipulation, and you will be able to find out if there is any manipulator in your life.

Any relationship can become abusive or emotionally manipulative even though manipulation is mostly talked about in romantic relationships' context. Relationships with manipulators may include relationships with abusive or toxic parents, overbearing or narcissistic partners, bosses, neighbors, roommates, friends, or in-laws. While you will likely not be emotionally manipulated in all of these areas we have mentioned, it is important that you know the common signs of manipulation and learn how to respond to it if you find yourself in such a situation.

The eleven chapters of this book reveal 11 strategies that can help you identify and understand manipulation. You will learn how to resist manipulation and use psychology to improve your life. Let us dive into the first chapter.

# CHAPTER ONE:
## Understanding Manipulation

Manipulation is a type of emotional abuse that is used to influence, control, and exploit other individuals to one's advantage. Manipulation controls how a person thinks, feels, and behaves in order for the manipulative individual to achieve their aim.

It is natural for individuals in relationships to encounter problems as the relationship continues to grow. Sometimes, greed or emotions can cause these issues. Manipulation is one problem that can come up in any kind of relationship. You need to know the signs of manipulation and how to handle it when it surfaces in your relationships.

Manipulation can occur in casual or close relationships, but you will find manipulation more in relationships that are closely formed. It includes any attempt that someone makes to sway another person's emotions to make them feel or act a certain way. It involves the exercise of influence over other people. Individuals who manipulate other people attack their emotional and mental sides to achieve their desires. The person who is manipulating others, and who is known as the manipulator, does so to create a power imbalance. The manipulator takes advantage of you to get privileges, control, power, and benefits. Manipulators use some common tricks to make you feel irrational and then increase the likelihood of having you do what they want you to do.

Although people display manipulative behavior every day, exhibiting a pattern of the tactics of manipulation is a sign of abuse. This may mean that the abuser has a serious mental health disorder, such as antisocial personality disorder or narcissistic personality disorder.

# Are You Being Manipulated?

Many manipulative individuals are highly skilled at getting you to believe that they are not doing anything that is wrong. If you suspect that you are being manipulated, what you should do is think about how that individual makes you feel after you interact with them.

One sign you can check for is if you are having feelings of confusion. When a person has pure, loving, and good intentions towards you, you will rarely be confused. Another sign to check for is if you feel fearful or hesitant to speak about your feelings openly or address your confusion. It is a red flag if you find it difficult to express your needs or ask a question without it turning into an argument. When an individual is defensive, it could be a sign that the person is feeling caught.

# Tactics Used in Manipulation

Manipulation tactics, also known as psychological or emotional manipulation tactics, give the manipulative individual a sense of control and power. Manipulation also ensures that the needs of the manipulative individual are met. A relationship is toxic if it has a pattern of manipulation tactics that is consistent. This pattern could also be a sign that a person is in a psychologically/emotionally abusive relationship.

Tactics of manipulation are the particular ways that an individual who is emotionally abusive attacks their victims. The individual uses the tactics to control their victim by eroding the victim's self-confidence and making them dependent on the abuser, thereby making it hard to leave the relationship. Common manipulation tactics include seeking control and gaslighting, but an abuser can control their victims through the use of many other tactics. You can use therapy to heal from trauma.

119

Manipulation can occur in a variety of forms. In fact, when someone behaves in a kind manner, they may be manipulating you, depending on what they hope to achieve.

## Manipulators have common traits. These traits include:

- They make you depend more on them by convincing you to give up an important thing.
- They are experts at using your insecurities against you.
- They are aware of the weaknesses you have and they know how to exploit those weaknesses.
- They don't stop manipulating you. They continue until you get yourself out of the situation.

## There are a variety of tactics that people use to manipulate others. Some other manipulation signs include:

### Endlessly judging you.

The manipulative individual does not mask their manipulation behind good fun or humor. In this situation, they go the route of ridiculing, judging, and dismissing you. They do their best to make you feel like what you are doing is wrong, and that you will never be good enough for them no matter what you do. The manipulator only focuses on negativity and never provides any constructive solutions.

### Denial and lying.

Manipulative individuals may tell their victims lies. After bombarding them with lies and they are caught, they may cover up with more lies or deny the lies.

### Intensifying insecurities.

Sadly, emotional manipulators are experts at noticing the insecurities of a person and intensifying them. The manipulator targets an individual's sense of shame, which is a feeling of inadequacy within the individual. Since shame is an emotion that is painful that many individuals avoid, triggering their shame encourages them to do what the manipulator wants so that they can avoid feeling it in the future.

The manipulator is an expert at playing on an individual's insecurities. They use this tactic to attack your weaknesses and increase your feelings of insecurity. They feel like they are psychologically superior when they make you look bad. The manipulator uses the tactic of knowing your sensitivities or unique triggers and uses them against you. Some individuals are experts at studying people and knowing the exact buttons to press to manipulate them. For instance, if you had a self-absorbed or selfish parent as a child and you didn't feel important because they were accusing you of being selfish, it would be a tactic that manipulators can use. The manipulator can use this because it will affect a deep childhood wound that you have had and it will make you question yourself and you will become motivated to do what will not make you appear selfish.

This tactic is quite popular among advertisers. A cosmetic company might make an individual feel old or unattractive. This tactic is also used in interpersonal relationships. For example, a person may make their romantic partner start thinking that they can never be loved by anybody else.

### The silent treatment.
Although it is normal for an individual to verbally and emotionally shut down if they are getting overwhelmed emotionally, a manipulator can also use this as a tactic to manipulate someone. A manipulative individual will shut down connections and communication as a form of punishment. This may include withholding affection, intimacy, or any form of communication.

## Changing the rules midway.
The manipulator might change a situation's rules midway through just to stop the victim from becoming successful. The rules could be something like highlighting elements that disqualify your success or

giving additional stipulations that you need to be successful. A manipulative individual keeps the other individual in a constant state of chasing the manipulator for their approval by using this tactic.

## Withholding some truths.

A manipulator will manipulate the facts. They will blame you, make excuses, lie to you, or withhold some truths and strategically share some facts about them. When they do this, it makes them feel that they are in charge and have power over you. They also feel like they are becoming superior intellectually.

## Making comparisons.

A manipulator can compare you to another individual to provoke you. They may make you feel insecure or make you feel like everyone else is doing that particular thing that you are not doing, but it is the manipulator who actually wants you to do that thing. They may compare you with a specific person, which can be annoying. They may even get other people to pressure you into doing a certain thing or getting a certain emotion out of you.

## The triangulation tactic.

Triangulation is when a third individual is brought in to sway the side that wins when two people disagree. Triangulation is used by a manipulative individual to ensure that their side emerges the winner of an argument. They can achieve this by floating the information to make it more in favor of their side or choosing a third individual that they know will agree with them.

This makes the victim question the manipulative individual less frequently, and then they eventually put an end to asking the manipulator questions. The victim's feelings of isolation can also be increased with this, and this increases the victim's dependence on the manipulative individual.

## Switching attention from themselves.

When there is an argument about a person's behavior, the person may switch the attention from themselves and change the subject by attacking their critic. This switching of attention may be the person saying something like, Well, what about your poor parenting skills? Or they may say, what about your drug abuse? In this case, the manipulative person takes the attention away from themselves to their partner's poor parenting skills or drug abuse.

## The advantage of location.

A person who is manipulating you will attempt to get you out of your comfort zone and take you to a place you find unfamiliar and where they will be in control.

## Love Bombing to build trust and intimacy.

A manipulator might control another individual's behavior through intense emotional connection.

For instance, an individual who is abusive may try to manipulate someone by making a romantic relationship move very quickly. They may display loving gestures to their victims to the point that they become overwhelmed with it or they may engage in love bombing to make their victim feel indebted and let down their guard.

Love bombing is when an individual bombards someone with intense emotions, affection, and excess energy and time. It may include spending a large part of one's energy and time pleasing the victim, making elaborate declarations of how one admires the victim, and giving the victim gifts. A manipulative individual quickly builds trust and intimacy with the victim through love bombing. The victim's natural desire to feel appreciated and wanted is preyed upon by the manipulator and it becomes a tool to increase devotion of the victim to them.

## The gaslighting tactic.

Gaslighting is when a person makes you question yourself, including your feelings, sanity, trust in yourself, memory, and even your own identity. This may be manipulating situations to make you doubt yourself or the abuser calling you crazy. A manipulative individual does this to make you automatically trust them and do what they ask you to do without asking them any questions, thereby giving them power and control over you.

## Making generalizations.

When an individual's traits are applied to a whole group of people who are in the same demographic, it is known as generalization. For instance, a manipulator might say that all women pay more attention to themselves than their partners. When the manipulator says something like this, the victim is then encouraged to act in a way that the manipulator considers easiest to control or agreeable with them.

## Controlling your daily activities and life.

Manipulation's goal is to have more control over you. But apart from controlling your behavior and how you feel, the manipulative individual is also able to shape what your daily activities and life look like. This can include restricting the friends you can spend time with, preventing you from continuing your education or even controlling access to your money. The goal of the manipulator in controlling your daily activities is to ensure that you feel like you cannot make decisions without them or function without them.

## Giving diminishing or dismissive comments.

A manipulative individual can respond with a diminishing or dismissive comment when their victim makes a contribution that is valid during discussions in a group or when they achieve success. The manipulator does this to stay in control. It can be like giving reasons for why their victim's comment is unworthy of the consideration and attention of other people, or giving reasons for why the victim's success was not earned.

## The projection tactic.
This involves a psychological defense mechanism where an individual puts their desires, characteristics, or feelings onto another individual. When the victim advocates doing something for themselves or presents alternative activities, the manipulator might say something like, you are so controlling. They take what they want and feel and project it onto the victim to avoid the feeling associated with it or how it makes them look.

## Name-calling you.
A manipulative individual will often label the behavior of the victim or the victim's personality traits with negative verbiage. This is done to make the victim feel like they are not enough, and also to convince them that they do not deserve to be treated better. This usually begins in small ways that are not very offensive and then increases in frequency and intensity as the victim gets more used to the name-calling.

## Guilt-tripping you.
A manipulative individual guilt-trips you to change how you feel. They might say something like, "If you choose to go out to the movies with your friend tonight, I will feel sad and lonely." The long-term goal of the manipulator is to get you to discuss that thing with them first in the future before doing it again.

## Blaming their victim for the emotional abuse.
It is common for the manipulative individual to shut down a victim when they speak up about emotional abuse. They shut the victim down by telling them that they actually did something to earn the emotional manipulation they are experiencing. This then makes the victim

always second guess their actions as they want to avoid having a negative interaction with the manipulative individual.

## Changing the topic.

Changing topics is normal during conversations, but a manipulative individual uses this tactic to make an individual feel devalued or to punish an individual. When someone gives the victim a compliment or the victim makes a valid point during a conversation, a manipulative individual will change the topic of the discussion to prevent the victim from gaining any confidence.

An emotional manipulator makes the victim question their own intelligence and abilities by ensuring that the victim feels like no one else can praise them other than the manipulator.

## Treating you like you are less capable or a child.

A manipulative individual treats their victim like a child or like they are less capable. It is a form of gaslighting that reduces the trust that the victim has in themselves to take charge of responsibility.

It may be in the form of physically treating the victim like they are not capable of performing certain tasks, taking over a task from the victim when they are already in the middle of a task that they can do on their own, or talking down to the individual like they are not intelligent enough.

## Using coercion or threats.

When an individual uses threats to convince you or force you to do something, you are being emotionally manipulated. This manipulation could include threats to take away something that you consider valuable and important or threats to leave you if you refuse to do what the individual wants you to do. The manipulator might even threaten to hurt themselves.

Although they may just be saying it and not actually want to hurt themselves, you need to always take threats that involve self-harm seriously. This is important. It is important that you maintain your boundaries for emotional and physical safety, and it is also important that you encourage the manipulator to get professional help if they threaten to harm themselves.

### Constantly shifting the criteria.

This is when a manipulator constantly shifts the goalposts. They keep shifting the criteria you must meet to satisfy them. For instance, a bully may harass their colleague at work by using their colleagues' clothes as an excuse to do that. If the colleague changes clothes because of the harassment, the bully may say that the colleague won't deserve to get professional respect until they also change their accent, hairstyle, or some other trait.

These forms of emotional manipulation may be combined by a manipulator or the manipulator may alternate between them depending on the situation.

# Reasons for Manipulation

Not every manipulation is done with malicious intent, even when the manipulator's actions cause immense harm.

### The following are some common reasons people engage in tactics of manipulation:

### Absence of connection.

Some individuals use manipulation to control other people and treat these people as a means to an end. Sometimes, this is a sign that the individual has a personality disorder like a narcissistic personality.

### Absence of effective communication skills.

Some individuals may not be comfortable with direct communication. Others may be from homes where manipulative communication was used.

### Social needs.

There are some forms of manipulation that are beneficial and even normal. For instance, most people learn that being cheerful and friendly around co-workers is important to advance professionally.

### A way to avoid blame.

People use manipulation to avoid blame. Although some individuals avoid blame as a way to abuse another individual or control them, others avoid blame because they have low self-esteem, they fear judgment, or they struggle to face the shortcomings they have.

### Manipulation as a result of fear.

Fear may make people manipulate others. The fear of abandonment is one of such fears. This usually occurs during relationship fights or breakups.

Advertising, marketing, and other political or financial incentives. Many industries are dedicated to manipulating the emotions of people to change their minds and get them to purchase products, or convince them to vote for a certain candidate or political party.

Many manipulators do not have effective communication skills. Or they might have been punished by an influential figure because they expressed their wants or needs. For this reason, the original means for connecting becomes replaced by strategies that are centered around staying away from any sense of fault. It is achieved through refusing to be accountable for actions and indirect communication.

# Treatment for Manipulation

It can be difficult to identify manipulation or even admit when you are being manipulated. This is not your fault, and it can be hard for you to prevent it. But you can do some things that can help you reduce the emotional impact that manipulation can have on you.

### You can set boundaries in a relationship by doing the following:

- Set boundaries to tackle manipulation and look for how to let the manipulator know that you are aware that they are manipulating you, and that you no longer want to take part in the conversation.
- Communication should be specific, direct, and clear.
- Look for someone you trust, who is not being influenced by the manipulator, and ask them to give you advice concerning the situation.
- Know when manipulation should be addressed.

When you are able to identify manipulation, you have solved a large part of the problem. If it is a loved one that is manipulating you, it can be hard to seek help. But manipulation is capable of affecting your emotional well-being. So, finding a safe way to solve the problem is important.

If you have feelings of being manipulated by someone, whether the person is a friend, relative, co-worker, partner, or anyone else, getting help is important. And you need to get help, especially if you notice that the situation is abusive in any way. You can talk to a friend, therapist, relationship counselor, or trusted family member.

# CHAPTER TWO:
## Embracing Your Identities

Every one of us has multiple identities, and those identities continue competing for primacy in our heads. We could help make the world a better place by learning to celebrate our complex identities.

There are different groups that compete for our attention and even demand to have the top spot in our lives. That includes political parties that influence our choices, musical styles that influence lifestyles, and companies that attempt to make their brands part of us, not to mention the different claims to gender, racial, and group loyalty.

When a group considers you disloyal, it can have severe consequences, since human beings allocate resources such as welfare support and housing, and emotional resources like compassion and empathy, through their groups. During times of war, deciding which identity to be loyal to can be difficult because it can be a matter of life and death.

And yet, evidence shows that our world would be a more peaceful and better place if we had space for different identities in ourselves as well as other individuals. How can you do this and try not to elevate one over all the others during times of conflict?

### Take a look at the following tips:

### Multiple identities are normal.
For many generations, rich politicians have positioned themselves as "one of you," while putting up policies that only benefited a small number of people, who are also rich people. Individuals march in public for gender or racial equality while privately acting in ways that increase gender and racial inequality.

Most people won't see this as news but let it be a reminder that things are always not as simple as they might appear to be. When you call yourself a progressive, it does not mean that every action you take or every word you say leads to progress, and becoming a Christian does not mean that you have become free of sin. Some individuals claim that when you join a group it will bring you many privileges. But after joining the group, you notice that things are not the way they presented them to be. You discover that they have manipulated you into joining the group and doing things that are in their own interest and not in your best interest.

We are complex individuals. We have identities that are sometimes conflicting as well as impulses that can lead to behavior that contradicts the words we say. This is a normal thing. Although there might not be a group that you can join that will take away all the problems you have in your life and the problems in the entire world, a complex social life that welcomes multiple identities can give you enormous richness.

You can belong to different groups, and other people can also do the same. Life is made interesting when the multiple identities we have come together to shape our behavior and decisions.

## Separate likability from credibility

Every one of us has been there. You are walking down your street and see somebody walking past you with the exact shirt you are wearing and you feel an instant connection with the individual. You belong to the same group.

Having those feelings is not bad. Nothing is wrong with it. People are usually happy when they randomly find others like this, and this part of human life is charming. But during serious discussions, every one of us needs to be wary of commonalities that are not relevant to the present topic.

131

Whether you want to acknowledge it or you don't want to acknowledge it, you often prefer individuals who are similar in interests, personality, intellect, demographics, and education to you. But just because a person listens to the same music that you listen to does not mean that the opinion they have about gas prices is more valid than the opinion of another person who listens to music that you don't like.

For this reason, likability needs to be separated from credibility, and we need to watch out for bias that may be present within ourselves against random in-groups and for random in-groups.

**Find the truth.**
Everybody feels intense social pressure to act and think in ways that are consistent with group activities that are important.

One major warning sign is when you join a group and you feel compelled to mislead other people or lie, especially about other groups. When that compulsion to lie to go along with the herd is present, you need to tell yourself that the group is not you and you are not the group. And you need to remind yourself that you need to find the truth and what is accurate in the group.

You need to ask questions if the group is focused on outsiders.

Groups may face communal threats even though not all the threats they get are serious ones. Some threats might be imaginary.

Leaders who are hungry for power know that fear is a powerful tool used by manipulators. A leader may mobilize fear against another group of people or turn their people into a threat against another group, thereby helping them to rise to power.

Fear can be misused. So, how can you know that it is being misused?

First, you need to name the emotion and also acknowledge that you feel afraid because of what you heard. Watch the fear you have without judgment. You can ask yourself if your fear is of specific acts or if your fear is of a whole group of people. Are you threatened personally? Is there any evidence of the threat? Is there any evidence that shows they are not a threat? Do you have any identities in common? Can you look for other things in common with them that would lead to a reduction in the threat? How can you respond courageously to this potential threat? Do you share any goals? How can you replace your fear with courage?

You might discover that fear is baseless or you might discover that it is saying that there is a real threat. You can avoid being manipulated by paying attention to what is going on around you.

**Appreciate the multiple identities in others and in yourself.** When you identify with a group, there will be pressure to behave in some particular ways, and you will notice that you are usually supporting norms that the group has accepted and norms that are common in the group. But many of us usually identify with more than one group, and it's okay. We identify with different groups, values, and norms that sometimes come into conflict with each other. And even as they conflict with each other, they still combine to give us our identity.

If visitors from outside the town or a unique event is what activates a strong group identity, you will discover that there is a change in someone's personality. On Friday, a friend might be talking fast, swearing, and also teasing to show affection, but then come to church on Sunday and then become suddenly different and quiet.

Identity shifts are important to us. If you are spending time with your children at the playground, the social role of parenting in the midst of other parents is what your sense of self is linked to. If you travel to another country and then attend an international food festival, seeing the different foods on display from your country will make you feel strong ties to your roots. You might be a cyclist back in your country. So, when you go for a bike ride, it will make you identify as a member of the cyclist community. You will identify with surfers if you surf. You will also have times when you need to connect with other parents and then advocate for the common interests you have. A day might come when you connect with other surfers or cyclists for a personal cause as well.

These different identities which span across talents, values, strengths, interests, and social roles make up who we are.

That insight can be used by you as a way to connect effectively with other people, even if those people first appear to be outsiders. It is important that we appreciate the numerous social categories that exist. If you are not a cyclist or you don't surf, you might connect with another individual over parenthood. If you cannot connect over parenthood because you are not a parent, surfing might be a common thing for you and the other individual.

Beyond individual connection moments, research shows that when a group embraces individuals who are different and encourages their group members to embrace unique identities that exist beyond the self, they can make better decisions. Wherever you are in the world, no individual possesses an identity that is only limited to nationality. Multiple identities are multiple opportunities, and you need to see things this way instead of seeing the multiple identities as threats to unity.

# CHAPTER THREE:
## The World of Dark Psychology

This should not freak you out. It is possible to know beyond words what people intend to say. You can sense what they mean from their heart even when they say something else. Your personal, social, and work life will be significantly affected by your ability to read people correctly. When you have an understanding of how another individual is feeling, your communication style and message can then be adapted to make sure that the other individual receives the message in the best way possible. This is not that difficult. Although this may appear cliché, no special powers are needed if you want to read people.

Dark psychology is how people use psychological tactics to manipulate other people and control them. It is the study of human nature's dark side or the psychological mechanisms that make people engage in manipulative, harmful, or antisocial behaviors. This topic is both a disturbing and fascinating one that explores the reasons why some individuals abuse, cheat, lie, steal, or even kill others.

Dark psychology techniques have been used to manipulate and control people by individuals in positions of power. It has been in existence for centuries. Today, people often associate it with psychopaths, sociopaths, and narcissists as they often use these techniques to achieve their desires.

**Have you been longing to read people with tricks from psychology? The following tips will help you read individuals like a pro:**

**Notice people's appearance.**
Do your best to notice peoples' appearance when you are reading

them. Pay attention to the clothes they are wearing. Are they putting on a T-shirt and jeans, which signifies comfort? Or they are dressed for success, which shows that they are ambitious?

Are they wearing a pendant such as a Buddha or cross which means they have spiritual values? You can sense something from whatever they are wearing. Ensure that you notice any identity claims. Identity claims are deliberate statements people make about their goals, attitudes, values, etc. and they include things such as rings, tattoos, or a t-shirt with slogans. An important thing to remember about identity statements is that because the identity statements are deliberate, a lot of individuals assume you are being disingenuous and manipulative with them, but there is very little evidence concerning this. The thing is, people usually want to be known. And they will even do their best to be known even at the expense of looking good. If they have to make a choice between being seen authentically and being seen positively, they would choose to be seen authentically instead.

Also, some studies show that people can read psychological traits at least to a certain degree on an individual's face.

A person with higher extraversion levels had more protruding lips and nose, masseter muscles, and a chin that is recessive. On the other hand, a person with lower levels of extraversion has a face in which the area that is found around the nose seems to press against the person's face. These studies show that perhaps psychological traits can to a certain degree be read on the face of an individual, though more research is required to gain an understanding of this phenomenon.

## Stay open-minded and objective.
Before you start trying to read people, the first thing to do is to work on having an open mind. Your past experiences and emotions should not be allowed to influence your opinions and impressions.

136

If you are quick to judge people, you will misread them. So, you need to be objective when approaching every situation and interaction. You won't get the whole story about someone when you use logic alone. You need some other important forms of information as you will be able to learn to use them to read the non-verbal cues that individuals give off. If you want to see somebody clearly, you need to stay objective and be able to receive information neutrally and not distort it.

### Don't avoid small talk.

Maybe you don't feel comfortable with small talk. However, this can give you the opportunity to become familiar with the other individual.

Small talk makes it easy for you to watch closely how an individual behaves during normal situations. This can then be a benchmark that will help you accurately discover any of a person's behavior that is out of the ordinary. One error that individuals make when trying to read people is that they don't get a baseline of their normal behavior.

### Be attentive and notice people's posture.

You can learn a lot about an individual's attitude from their posture. The person is confident if they walk with their head held high. However, they may have low self-esteem if they walk in an indecisive manner.

When you are looking at a person's posture, see if the person walks in an indecisive manner as it means that they have issues with their self-esteem, or if they walk with their head held high as it indicates that they are confident.

### Pay attention to the words and tone a person uses.

When you are talking to an individual, pay attention to the words they use. When the person says "This is my third promotion," they are telling you that they have been promoted twice before. One thing you should know is that people like this often rely on other people to boost their self-image. They are hoping that you will praise them so that it can boost their self-image and make them feel good about themselves.

It is important that you also pay attention to the tone used. The tone a person uses and the volume of their voice can reveal a lot about their emotions. Vibrations are created by sound frequencies. When reading individuals, pay attention to how their voice tone affects you. Ask yourself if the person's tone feels soothing or if it is whiny, snippy, or abrasive.

## Pay attention to the physical movements they make.

People express their feelings more through their movements than their words. For instance, we often lean towards the people we like and move away from the people we do not like. One good sign is if a person is leaning in, their palms facing up, and hands out and open. This indicates that the person is connecting with you. If you notice that the individual is leaning away, it indicates that they are putting up a wall.

Another physical movement you can look out for is the crossing of legs or arms. If you notice that someone is crossing their legs or arms, it indicates anger, defensiveness, or self-protection. If a person is leaning in and you say something and they cross their arms all of a sudden, it means that you said something that the individual does not like.

On the other hand, if a person is hiding their hands, it indicates that the person is hiding something. But if you notice that the person is cuticle picking or lip biting, it indicates that they are in an awkward situation or trying to soothe themselves under pressure.

## Ask questions that are direct to receive a straight answer.

If you want to receive a straight answer, you have to avoid asking questions that are vague. Ensure that you don't interrupt when the individual is providing an answer to your question. Instead, observe their mannerisms as they speak. You can gain valuable insight into how an individual thinks from action words.

For instance, if someone says that they have decided to choose a particular brand, "decided" is the action word. The word shows that the person has weighed different options, the person is not impulsive, and they usually think things through. Action words help you understand how an individual thinks.

### Pay attention to your gut.
When you first meet someone, it is important to listen to your gut. Before you even get a chance to think, this will give you a visceral reaction. Your gut can help you know whether you are at ease or not with the individual.

They occur quickly, helping you know if you can trust people. They are your internal truth meter.

### Stay alert and notice flashes of insight.
Sometimes, there may be an ah-ha moment about someone. You need to pay attention because the insights come in a flash. We often miss it because we move rapidly on to the next thought and we lose these critical insights.

### Avoid assumptions.
When you make assumptions and are not sure of something, it can lead to misunderstanding. There may be more trouble if you simply make assumptions without having a full understanding of the other person. People can make errors when they make assumptions when reading others. One such error is not being conscious of biases.

For instance, if you simply assume that someone is angry, then whatever that person does or says will appear to be concealed anger to you. You don't have to jump to conclusions when your spouse doesn't watch your favorite TV show with you but goes to bed. Don't think that they don't want to spend time with you; they may just be tired and want to rest. If you want to read people like a pro, you need to keep your mind positive and open, and you also need to relax.

## Sense the individual's presence.
What this means is that you need to feel the emotional atmosphere surrounding you. Try to notice if someone you are reading has a presence that is making you back off if they have a friendly presence that pulls you closer to them, or if you face a wall. The energy we emit is referred to as presence, and it is not necessarily congruent with behavior or words.

## You can feel goosebumps.
You can have goosebumps when you resonate with individuals who inspire or move you. You can also have goosebumps if what an individual is saying strikes a chord within you. Music, movies, and moving experiences seem to trigger it.

Also, you can feel goosebumps when you experience deja vu, which is a recognition that you have known a person before, even though you have never met the person.

## Scan the overall behavior of the person.
People sometimes make the assumption that if a certain action is done, like when a person is looking down at the floor when having a conversation, it shows that they are anxious or nervous.

But familiarity with a person will help you know whether they are just relaxing when they look down on the floor or when they avoid eye contact. People have different ways in which they behave, and some of these behaviors that people have are simply mannerisms. This is what makes creating a baseline of the normal behavior of others helpful. Learn how you can identify any deviation from the usual behavior that a person has. When you discover that there is a change in their body language, pace, or tone, you will know that something is not right.

## Observe people's eyes.

Have you ever heard people say that the eyes are the doorway to people's souls? Our eyes transmit energies that are powerful. So, ensure that you carefully watch people's eyes. What do you see when you observe someone's eyes? Do you see a guarded, angry, or mean person? Or do you see a caring person? A person's eyes can reveal whether they are telling the truth or lying. When you look at someone's pupil size, you can also tell if they like something.

## Practice studying people.

You will become perfect with practice. When you practice studying people, you will be able to read them more accurately with time. Do this exercise where you practice putting talk shows on mute while watching them. Observing their actions and facial expressions will help you see what individuals are feeling when they are speaking, without hearing anything they are saying. Then, put the volume on and watch again to see if your observation was right.

## Try to interpret the person's facial expressions.

Unless you have mastered the poker face, you will usually have your emotions showing on your face. You can interpret facial expressions in a variety of ways. They include:

When you notice that deep frown lines are forming, it means that the individual is overthinking or worried. On the other hand, you will notice crow's feet, which are the smile lines of joy in an individual who is truly laughing.

One other thing to watch out for is if the person's lips are pursed, which can signal contempt, anger, or bitterness. Also, when a person is grinding their teeth or has a clenched jaw, it means they are tense.

## The following is a classification of smiles in psychology today:

**The reward smile:** This is when the individual's lips are pulled directly upwards, eyebrows lift, and dimples at the sides of the mouth. This shows positive feedback.

**The affiliative smile:** This is when the individual presses their lips together and at the same time has little dimples at the side of their mouth. It signifies liking and friendship.

**The dominance smile:** This is when the individual's upper lip is raised with their cheeks being pushed upwards, there is a deepening of the indentation between the nose and the mouth, the upper lids are raised, and there is a wrinkling of the nose.

It is important that you know how to read people. Reading people makes you sensitive to people's needs and struggles. Learning this skill will help you boost your EQ. Anyone can read people. You only need to be aware of what to look for.

# Analyzing Individuals with Dark Psychology

Are you triggered? Is somebody constantly showing raging anger? Are you being triggered and continuously taken advantage of? Do you frequently get anxious and feel somebody is emotionally insensitive? You may be searching for something to see if the individual is trustworthy or not.

Studies show that whenever you see an individual that has a dark personality, there is an amygdala activation and your mind and body become instantly aware.

The amygdala, which becomes active whenever a person's body perceives a threat, is a flight and fight response center of the brain. The brain learns these traits over our human race's evolution. So, you will often get triggered when dealing with individuals with dark personalities.

When you use dark psychology, you will see that it is capable of helping you know why people make certain decisions or behave the way they do. You can use dark psychology to predict a person's future behavior by studying their past behavior. You can use this in a variety of situations such as predicting the performance of employees or predicting the behavior of customers. You can also use dark psychology to identify patterns in an individual's behavior that you may not notice at first glance. You will understand why people take certain actions and make certain decisions when you study the patterns over time. Also, dark psychology makes it possible for you to see how a person's overall behavior or decision-making process can be affected by different factors.

You will find dark psychology important when it comes to understanding human behavior and analyzing their behavior from a scientific perspective. It makes it possible for researchers to gain a deeper understanding of why individuals behave the way they do by paying attention to and studying over time the processes that are both conscious and unconscious. When researchers utilize techniques of dark psychology, they are able to better predict future behaviors from past behaviors and also identify patterns in the behavior of individuals that may not be noticed immediately. A greater potential for unlocking the mysteries that surround human thought processes comes with the ever-increasing popularity of dark psychology, and this could benefit every one of us for many years to come.

Dark Psychology combines psychopathy, narcissism, and Machiavellianism. Therefore, you need to essentially analyze these factors when you want to analyze people with dark psychology. Some individuals are evil-minded. They see life as a chessboard, and they use the individuals around them as pawns. They will do anything to win a trophy.

These cold-blooded toxic and cunning people will strip your identity away, give you an image, and also give you a cheerleader role that you will play for them. They are your masters and saviors.

The dark psychology triad is about three personality traits that are connected to manipulative and malicious behaviors.

## The personality traits include:

### The Machiavellianism trait.

Machiavellianism consists of a set of personality traits associated with deceptive and manipulative behaviors. It is named after Niccolo Machiavelli, who was an Italian Renaissance politician known for his deceitful and cunning political strategies. People high in Machiavellianism are skilled at navigating social situations to their advantage. These people are often strategic and manipulative.

You would come in contact with a person or the other in social life or the workplace with such personalities who manipulate, trigger, or irritate you. This person may be your romantic partner, colleague, or boss. You may be trying to learn how to identify people with dark psychology because you suspect that there is a person in your life with a dark personality. Machevallianism, which is a manipulation trait, is something a dark triad would have. You will also feel that you are constantly being manipulated by the individual whom you believe has a dark personality.

Is manipulation and deception the same? Deception and manipulation may get you confused. Are you being manipulated?

Firstly, we need to understand what causes the so-called dark personality.

## The narcissism trait.

This personality trait is characterized by a need for validation and admiration, a lack of empathy for other individuals, and an inflated sense of self-importance. Narcissists believe that they should be given special treatment because they are special. Their sense of entitlement causes them to mistreat other people and exploit them to achieve their own goals. They may also be resentful, arrogant, and envious.

If you are concerned about getting an analysis of a dark personality, you may have presumed that the individual you are trying to analyze may be a narcissist. Two particular reasons exist for it; one is that the internet is filled with ideas, videos, and articles about narcissism, and the second is the attractiveness, charmingness, charm, and aura of the narcissist. Narcissists are manipulators.

The difference between narcissism and a dark triad and psychology is a dark personality looks for an object's benefit like work, sex, or money, while a narcissist often looks for a victim and seeks your emotional energy.

A dark personality squeezes the resources you have, while a narcissist drains your emotions. You are dealing with a dark triad when an individual has some traits that are matching with a narcissist, but many traits are not.

Codependency syndrome is an important character trait that attracts narcissists. Codependency involves your personality vulnerability through which you become dependent on a narcissist. So, your own vulnerabilities are one thing you should look out for.

An online codependency test can help you find out if you are codependent or not. If you have a moderate codependency scale, you have a lower probability of being with a narcissist, and so if you are with a person, who may be triggering you, then the individual has a higher likelihood of having multiple dark personality traits.

## The psychopathy trait.

This personality disorder is marked by a deficiency in empathy, remorse, and conscience. Psychopaths often have high impulsivity and a superficial charm. These people may exhibit aggressive, antisocial, and violent behaviors without thinking about the consequences of their actions. They may also be parasitic, irresponsible, and callous.

Understanding gender differences is one essence of dark psychology analysis. The individual who has triggered you to search for dark psychology is probably someone who is bossy.

You might feel like the bossy person is excessively dominating you. Females that have a high level of psychopathy, and who are also in a position of leadership have a strong negative correlation with transformational leadership. So, the person is not able to transform an organization or system effectively even when they are bossy.

Therefore, If a female is bossy and is in a leadership position, but no visible transformation or visible impact exists, then she may be high on the dark triad.

## Impulsivity and dominance.

Impulsivity and fearless dominance are two important traits of psychopathy.

If you have witnessed impulsive reactions that were sudden and the individual appears to be more fearless than the people around you, it means that the probability of a very high trait of psychopathy is high. In addition, an individual who has a high psychopathy trait has an affinity for pain. They like to either receive pain or give pain. This involves emotional pain, which is associated with narcissists, as well as physical pain.

So, if you have witnessed the individual causing physical boundary breaching, throwing things, and taking or giving physical pain, you may be dealing with an individual with a dark triad and personality.

## Using Biology to Analyze Dark Psychology

Knowing the biology of a dark personality trait is also important because biology is responsible for many of their behaviors. Since a distinct different genetic and brain pattern is present in any mental disorder, a distinct biological pattern is bound to be present. One key trait of a dark personality is the desire to achieve more. This makes them have low pre-frontal cortex activation as well as low consciousness. A behavior's consequence is analyzed by the prefrontal cortex.

Our consciousness hormone is serotonin. Therefore, PFC is activated by this hormone. Hence an individual with a dark psychology, dark personality, and the dark triad will have low consciousness as well as serotonin. This is referred to as the serotonin syndrome.

### You need to know the following:

1. Dopamine and serotonin hormones are responsible for neuroplasticity and link the cerebellum, prefrontal cortex, and hippocampus. Therefore, the DTP possesses very low dopamine and serotonin. And they are always moody and unhappy.

147

2. Their thermal regulation is gone as a result of the lack of serotonin. Therefore, they are cold-blooded and warmth is absent when you are touched by them.

3. The HPA axis is activated by the midbrain and has high adrenaline. Therefore, they are angry, aggressive, and raging with expressed or suppressed violence.

4. Research has shown that people who are pathological liars lack prefrontal cortex activation. The mid-brain mostly manages it.

5. Acidosis is caused by hypothermic blood. This leads to tissue necrosis. So, several skin problems continue to exist. They have the feeling of cold, which makes them hydrophobic, thereby resulting in avoiding washing and baths.

6. Because the somatic nervous system is also regulated by serotonin, there is poor muscle control. An inability to do small works like threading a needle, tremors, or a weak handshake.

7. Ectopic heartbeat and palpitations are caused by hypothermia. So, they get very anxious and are always afraid.

8. Because high neuron activation, which gets impaired as a result of serotonin deficiency and leads to minerals being absorbed in low amounts, is needed by gut wall peristalsis, physical strength, muscles, and bones are reduced.

9. Serotonin makes it hard for them to sleep early.

10. They are skeptical of reality as a result of a lack of PFC activation. This makes them stalkers and detectives.

11. Vasoconstriction is caused by high adrenaline, resulting in very high blood pressure.

12. They do their best to use confidence to overcome this fear. This mask comes off when they are under stress and their response becomes violent.

13. The kidney is unable to remove such a large amount of waste. Therefore, stinking body odor is developed, thereby becoming toxic.

14. They don't have any solid memory, so they create stories to make sense of their life. It is only those things that satisfy their stories that they remember.

15. A hypertensive father, who is highly aggressive, and a depressed mother who made some compromises to maintain the family, leading to DTP.

### Using biology to analyze dark psychology:

- Their body temperature may be low, and when they are given a body touch such as a handshake, the handshake may feel very cold.
- They may be highly conscious of their image, thereby their brand of consciousness may be very high.
- They may suffer from some allergies such as itching.
- They may suffer from hydrophobia, thereby making them avoid baths.
- Their natural body odor may be very bad and they may resort to using fragrance.
- They may have hypertension.
- They may not be sleeping early at night, and dark circles would be seen in their eyes as a result of staying awake till late at night.

# Using Behavioural and Social Traits to Analyze Dark Personality

The signature of all the criminals is pretty much the Dark Triad. Personality(DTP). These individuals convince themselves that they are without guilt and they are good people, while they are full of lies and manipulation. What they say and do differ greatly.

As long as you agree to what they want, they are very nice. However, when you start to disagree with what they want, they get angry and shun you down with their anger and words.

They make you afraid. They have extreme envy, jealousy, and hatred. They do their best to act as the victims in every situation. They blame you for everything, and they shame-trip and guilt-trip you. They don't really feel sorry when they say they are sorry. This is because serotonin, which connects the entire brain, is needed for feeling.

They find it hard to do something for long as they get easily bored. They start doing something but never complete it. They are afraid of reality. They stalk you to get all the information.

They will always appear smart and silently instigate you against those close to you and your loved ones. They will try to look for shortcuts to achieve success. You will experience a kind of chill feeling and your gut will tell you. Yet, you will not pay attention and listen to anybody.
So, an individual who finds it boring to do the same work over and over again, and who is always seeking out new things that they can do to take away their boredom, may have a dark Psychology.

Once you have DTP, there is no going away as it is an addiction. Your mind stays hostage forever.

Are you hoping that they will change? This disorder is clinically irreversible. Your serotonin shouldn't be depleted by you hating, hoping, and getting hurt. You need to run as far as you can.

# Understanding Manipulation and Dark Psychology in Relationships

The field of psychology covers a variety of topics, all looking to elucidate the human mind and human behavior's complexities. While a large part of this work is focused on positive elements such as personal development as well as mental health and well-being, a darker side also exists in psychology. The realm of dark psychology is this shadowy corner. But what exactly is it, and what is the manifestation like in our daily lives?

Dark psychology involves the scientific study of human behavior's darker aspects. The human behavior includes deceit, control, manipulation, coercion, and persuasion. It usually investigates actions that are ethically and morally wrong, especially those actions that are aimed at harming other people or exploiting them. It is sometimes connected to studies about "dark triad" personality traits, and they include psychopathy, Machiavellianism, and narcissism.

The idea behind dark psychology is to have a full understanding of these behaviors that are harmful and not to glorify them. When you study them, you will be able to come up with ways to identify and protect yourself and others against them.

Manipulation is an important part of dark psychology. Manipulative behaviors that people display may range from emotional manipulation that is subtle to tactics that are blatant and overt. Guilt-tripping, playing the victim, psychological bullying, gaslighting, or using fear as a control tactic, are some of these actions.

A case of manipulation and dark psychology might involve an individual in a position of power, such as the CEO of a company, using the position they have as the CEO to influence or control their subordinates in an unfair manner. This could be in the form of playing favorites, subtly threatening job security, or exploiting the employees' personal information for their own advantage.

Manipulators usually understand human emotions deeply and use this knowledge that they have to play with the feelings of others and control the way they respond. This can lead to severe psychological and emotional damage to the individual who is on the receiving end of those tactics.

Dark psychology is a field of psychology that is based on understanding, analyzing, as well as manipulating the behavior of people. It has been in existence for centuries, but its popularity is increasing as the world becomes more interconnected and complex.

The study of the behavior of humans from a scientific perspective is referred to as dark psychology. It involves gaining insight into how individuals think and act by using research methods such as surveys, psychological tests, interviews, and observational studies. It considers both conscious as well as unconscious processes in order to have a better understanding of why people take the actions they take.

Dark psychology is based on two main principles at its core. They include persuasion and manipulation. Persuasion involves trying to convince a person to change their opinion of something through emotional appeals or logical arguments, while manipulation involves gaining control over another individual through the use of your influence or power. Manipulation usually relies on coercion or deception. Both manipulation and persuasion are used in dark psychology.

Using psychological tactics to influence decision-making or behavior is another major concept in dark psychology. These psychological tactics can vary from subtle suggestions or hints to more overt types of manipulation like fearmongering. The idea is always to get another person to do the particular thing you want them to do, not minding if it is not in their own best interests.

Dark psychology is used in many areas, and it is used in both professional and personal settings. It can be used personally for self-advancement purposes or it can be used to manipulate other people for one's advantage. It can be used professionally for deal negotiations, sales techniques, and marketing purposes. Law enforcement officers also use dark psychology during interrogations and politicians use it during their speeches and debates in order to persuade the audience in the direction they want them to go.

There are numerous ways in which dark psychology can manifest in relationships. These ways include gaslighting, manipulation, emotional abuse, or even physical violence. These tactics are usually used by abusers to control their partners and exert power over their partners, thereby creating an environment that is toxic.

One partner in a relationship may control the other partner through emotional manipulation. For instance, they may constantly belittle the feelings of their partner, telling them that they are too sensitive or overreacting, or even making them feel guilty because they expressed their needs. A power imbalance is created in the relationship, and this can cause emotional damage.

In a case such as this, the victim often feels confused, powerless, or trapped, doubting their memories or experiences as a result of the tactics of the manipulator. Understanding dark psychology's signs can make it possible for people to spot such harmful behaviors if they exist in their relationships and then get help.

# Manipulation Techniques of Dark Psychology

### Intimidation and fear.
This can be likened to the bully who threatens to take a person's lunch money. They use fear to achieve their desire instead of using their words to get it. This is not a good way to play.

### Guilt-tripping as a technique of dark psychology.
Has a close friend ever made you feel guilty whenever you were unable to hang out? Your friend might say something like, "I think I will just spend time alone at home then." This is a guilt trip.

## The love-bombing and devaluation technique.

This is when you get a ton of compliments from a person, and then they start making criticisms about whatever you do. It's often hurtful and confusing, and often like a roller coaster of emotions.

## Distraction and misdirection.

Imagine this like a magician who keeps you distracted with what they are doing with one hand and it takes your focus away from what the other hand is doing. Individuals using this technique might decide to do something dramatic or change the subject to distract you and take your focus away from the present thing that is happening.

## Gaslighting as a technique of dark psychology.

Imagine if a person began to question your memories and they tell you that events that you know happened and clearly remember never took place. This is what gaslighting is. It works just like a magic trick made to cause you to doubt your memories.

Gaslighting is a common manipulative tactic linked to dark psychology. It is a kind of psychological abuse whereby an individual makes another individual question their memories, perception of reality, or sanity.

Gaslighting involves making an individual always second-guess themselves, even questioning their reality or judgment. The people who use dark psychological tactics have this as a powerful tool in their arsenal, thereby leading to confusion and immense emotional distress.

Gaslighting might happen in a romantic relationship where one of the partners in the relationship always questions the other partner's memory. For example, the partner may deny that some events took place or they may even deny that they made certain promises, insisting that their partner is the one overreacting or misremembering. With time, this can make the victim start doubting their own sanity or memory.

### Control of information.
Have you ever been in a position where everybody else appeared to know what was going on but your friend kept you in the dark about those things? That is control of information. This is just like the case where you are the last person to hear the gossip that has been around, but on a scale that is more serious.

### Exploitation of affection and trust.
Do you have a friend who knows you would do anything to make them happy, and they use that to exploit your affection and trust to their advantage? It's like having a secret weapon they can use to get their way.

### Endless criticisms.
Picture an individual who continues to make snide comments about you, but later turns around and pretends like they are the only one who really understands you. It's just like having an individual who is your friend but continues to point out that there is spinach in your teeth but doesn't offer you a mirror to see it.

# Dark Psychology and the Evil Label

It is important that we remember that psychology when looked at as a discipline seeks to gain an objective understanding of human behavior without applying labels such as "evil" or "good."

Dark psychology studies tendencies and behaviors that are undoubtedly unethical and harmful, but when we label dark psychology as "evil," the complex issues at hand could be oversimplified. Instead, it is best viewed as a tool to understand human behavior's harmful aspects to mitigate or prevent their effects.

The "evil" label is usually subjective and it can depend on personal or cultural values. However, the actions often associated with dark psychology have a harmful impact. For example, a company head who knowingly spreads false rumors to boost their own status and undermine competitors is displaying harmful and unethical actions even though their actions may not be necessarily "evil."

## Facts of Dark Psychology

• Dark psychology is connected to the "dark triad" of personality traits, which include psychopathy, Machiavellianism, and narcissism. Individuals who possess these traits usually show tendencies for deceit, manipulation, and a lack of empathy. Dark psychology's relevance in understanding human behavior that is harmful is demonstrated by the facts around dark psychology. For instance, an individual displaying the dark triad's traits may regularly demonstrate behavior that is manipulative. This individual may deceive other people for their own personal gain, show a sense of entitlement, and show little remorse for their behavior.

• Dark psychology encompasses unethical and harmful behaviors, even though it is not evil per se.

• Dark psychology represents harmful behaviors collections that are widely studied, and this field is not formally recognized within psychology.

• Tactics of dark psychology like gaslighting are capable of causing individuals to question their own perception of reality.

Dark psychology reminds us of human behavior's complexities. It highlights the importance of recognizing and understanding destructive and manipulative behaviors to protect society and individuals from their effects. Although the field is dark, it is capable of shedding light on the things we need to do to implement a safer, healthier society.

# Dark Psychology Benefits

1. Dark psychology makes it possible for you to understand why individuals do the things they do.

2. Improvement in the ability to detect manipulation, deception, or coercion by other individuals, and defend against them. It also includes the ability to shield oneself from exploitation or harm.

3. Enhanced competencies and skills in different domains that require psychological knowledge as well as insight, such as education, security, or law enforcement.

4. Increase in understanding of behavior and nature, especially the often ignored or hidden darker aspects. The benefits also include an increase in awareness.

Dark Psychology Harmful Effects

Dark psychology can also be harmful to people and society even though it can be intriguing and fascinating.

5. It can lead to an increase in violence and aggression: Individuals who practice dark psychology may lack remorse, empathy, or conscience for their actions. They may see other people as objects or tools that they can use for their own gain, and pay no attention to these people's feelings or rights. They may have narcissism, superiority, or a sense of entitlement as well that makes them harm others and feel justified for doing that. This can result in homicide, criminal activity, or antisocial behavior in the dark psychology perpetrators.

6. It can affect rationality and decision-making: Individuals who are exposed to tactics of dark psychology such as persuasion, misinformation, or propaganda can be influenced to take actions that are against their own values or best interests. These individuals can be swayed by fear-mongering, false promises, or emotional appeals, and lose their independent and critical thinking ability. This can lead to guilt, regret, or poor choices in the dark psychology victims.

7. It can damage relationships and trust: Individuals who use techniques of dark psychology such as gaslighting, lying, or emotional manipulation can destroy the trust and bond they have developed with

other individuals. They can cause others to doubt their judgments, feelings, and reality, and create a sense of insecurity and confusion. This can lead to anxiety, low self-esteem, emotional distress, and depression in the dark psychology victims.

## Protecting Yourself from the Negative Effects of Dark Psychology

**Stay informed and aware:** The first thing to do to shield yourself from the negative effects that dark psychology can cause is to be aware that it exists and know its signs. Study the different strategies and techniques, such as persuasion, deception, hypnosis, gaslighting, and lying, that the practitioners of dark psychology use to manipulate other people. Learn how to identify and resist these tactics. Look for reliable information sources and verify any facts or claims before accepting them.

**Be confident and assertive:** After becoming informed and aware, the next step to take if you want to protect yourself from the negative effects of dark psychology is to be proactive as well as confident in your own values and identity. Do not allow other people to tell you what to think or do. They should not define you. Stand up for your rights and what you believe in. Express your feelings and opinions respectfully and clearly. Feel free to disagree with others or say no when necessary. Trust your intuition and instincts, and do not give other people the opportunity to make you doubt your reality or yourself.

**Be supportive and selective:** The next step after being confident and assertive is to be supportive and selective in your social circles and relationships. Choose respectful, trustworthy, and honest individuals, and those who care for you and others. Avoid abusive, manipulative, or dishonest individuals, or those who are toxic towards you or others. Get support from your family members, friends, or professionals if you feel that dark psychology is affecting you or if you need help handling the effects of dark psychology.

The field of dark psychology is controversial and complex and it brings up many moral and ethical questions. Approaching it with caution as well as critical thinking is important. Balancing it with positive psychology is also important. Positive psychology has to do with studying human nature's positive aspects. It focuses on topics such as resilience, gratitude, happiness, purpose, compassion, well-being, optimism, altruism, resilience, and meaning. Its aim is to promote social good and human flourishing.

# CHAPTER FOUR:
## Making the Best of Body Language

Body language is something powerful that can be used in the workplace. You just need to use it to your advantage. We will discuss how this nonverbal communication tool can be used in the workplace.

There are different things to look at when conducting yourself, whether it is in your workplace or for an interview. Verbal as well as nonverbal communication plays a major role in this. Perhaps body language is a nonverbal form of communication that is very important. It is easy to notice when a person displays body language that is friendly or hostile, but how can these cues be used to your advantage?

It is important that you first understand what makes body language important. A large percentage of communication that humans make is nonverbal. What this means is that, when you smile with others, you will easily develop an instant connection with them than when you simply say "hello." Using hand gestures can place more emphasis on something than simply using words. And when you stand and your feet are in a wide stance, it shows that you are confident, and this subconsciously makes you be trusted by listeners. Body language has the capability to convey our intentions and emotions in ways that words are not able to. It is a powerful tool.

Body language usually sends a strong message, and it might even send a message that is stronger than the words you are saying aloud. This means that we can use our bodies to control how people perceive us. It is not only our voices we can use for communication.

You need to know some things pertaining to the messages you are sending and you also need to know how to use the signals you get to your advantage. You need to first know that displaying emotion is something that is more complicated than the frown or smile on your face. It has to do with the way you move the whole of your body.

If you want to convey success by using your body language, you can do it through the strategies mentioned below. The way you use your hands and the way you stand matter.

Your hands are capable of speaking for you, and sometimes, they can even do the speaking more than your mouth can. If you are experiencing difficulty establishing and expressing your confidence, you can try using non-verbal cues.

So, it is not a must that you must display complete determination with your body language every time. But these are postures and gestures that you should do your best to avoid. Mixed signals might be sent to an impressionable audience through these negative movements.

Has anybody ever told you that you look defensive or unfriendly whenever you cross your arms? This happens to be true. You need to be physically open as it can make people see that you are open-minded, happy, or confident. Paying attention to physical cues to know when a person is telling you lies is also helpful.

To portray emotional closeness and empathy, you need to mirror the individual you are having a conversation with.

Although smiling makes you appear more approachable and friendly, the different nature of showing your teeth has psychological effects. Ensure that you are not staring at the person you are communicating with awkwardly as eye contact is important.

**Here are some ways you can start using body language to your advantage:**

## 1. Using eye contact.

When you make eye contact with an individual, both at the time you are listening and speaking, it shows that you are fully present in the conversation you are having with the person. Many people have the desire to be heard, so when they believe that you are fully engaged with them, it creates a sense of comradery and warmness. Making eye contact with a person shows that you are not hiding anything.

Our eyes can also help us detect what people like. To do this, it is important that you look at the pupil size in combination with the direction in which a person is looking. Think about a recent visit you had to a restaurant. When you were deciding on what to eat, did you know straight away what you wanted to eat? Such decisions can be difficult. For instance, when making a choice between what food you should eat and what food you actually want to eat. One interesting thing is that when you have a difficult decision to make, your eyes will most likely move back and forth between the options for the food you are considering eating, and your last gaze is often at the option you finally go with. By paying attention to where an individual is looking, the options they consider can be known.

The eyes also have the ability to let us know if we experience an unpleasant thing. Therefore, if you want to find out whether a person is feeling good or bad, you can do this by considering the situation and their eyes as well.

Looking into someone's eyes can help you read their mind. How can you know what is going on in someone's mind? How can you get access to the information on their mind?
Many artists have used the phrase, "I can see it clearly in your eyes." Even if someone is trying to hide how they feel, they can't stop their eyes from telling the truth.

Looking at someone's eyes is a powerful thing, and it can help you read their mind. So how can you read someone's mind through their eyes?

If you want to know what is on someone's mind, you need to look deeply into their eyes and look for any changes that are occurring in their pupil size.

In addition to getting information from people, our eyes also send sensitive signals that other individuals can pick up on. You can determine emotions, such as anger and fear, just by looking at people's eyes. The eyes are also capable of revealing whether someone is telling the truth or telling lies.

Does this mean that individuals can read whatever is on someone's mind by looking at the person's eyes and that they need to look at only the signal from the eyes to get the required information?

There is no doubt that our "mind-reading abilities" are dependent on the context. You need to know that you might read the eyes of your loved ones better than the eyes of strangers because you can easily understand your loved one's facial expressions and know when they are surprised, angry, happy, and so on. Having evidence is important. It is the key that helps us make better assessments of the feelings of other people. But because individuals are unable to control how their pupil reacts, the eyes are an important source of information that is often under-used. They are capable of helping us develop better bonds with the people around us.

You might not be able to read someone's exact thoughts from just looking at the person's eyes. This ensures that the privacy of our thoughts is maintained. But eyes reveal to us much more than our assumptions tell us. Unlike our mouths, our eyes do not lie.

## 2. Stand straight and maintain a good posture.

While it is important to stand straight and maintain a good posture, this is important in your place of work. The reason is that it increases the power of your voice and also helps you appear confident. When you stand up straight, more air gets into your lungs as well as through your abdomen, thereby maximizing your voice's sound and reinforcing your confidence.

## 3. Put your hand over your heart to emphasize a point.

Placing a hand over your heart to make a specific point is another hand gesture that creates a feeling of honesty and trustworthiness. This is the case because a lot of cultures believe this gesture is displayed by a person whose intentions appear to be genuine, or it is displayed by someone pledging allegiance or giving their word of honor. Listeners will likely feel more bonded and closer to you as a result of the subconscious idea that you are an open book, and they will also have a higher likelihood of trusting your intentions.

## 4. Gesture with an open hand.

When you are using hand gestures to convey a message, ensure that you avoid pointing with your finger. This is because when you point at other people, some cultures consider it rude and associate it with the allocation of blame. The person listening to you could feel like the object of criticism or feel accused, even if that is not what you mean. This can result in defensive and negative feelings that can get the point you are trying to make jeopardized. Instead, you can gesture with an open hand.

## 5. Subtly Mirror your listener's stance.

You don't have to copy every one of your listener's gestures. They will consider this creepy. But you can subtly mirror their speaking speed or stance as it will make them feel more accepted. Why is this so? Because, people tend to mirror the habits of the individuals that they like, and they do it subconsciously.

Although this information may appear to be a lot, you don't have to be an expert to benefit from nonverbal communication. You just need to know the body language basics and you will be able to avoid errors and interact well with people. Once you are confident in your skills and abilities, people will easily see your professional value.

# CHAPTER FIVE:
## Manipulation in the Workplace

You can identify dark personality traits in the workplace and communicate better with your colleagues.

### You need to know the following:

• Manipulation in the workplace can happen when a colleague at work or supervisor uses coercion, shame, guilt, or other tactics to exploit another person on the team.

• If your company's CEO is a manipulator in the workplace, look for behavioral qualities and traits that show that your CEO might possess dark personality traits.

• Characteristics that can show that a person has manipulative tendencies include dark personality traits such as psychopathy, Machiavellianism, and narcissism.

• When you learn to spot dark personality traits, you will find it beneficial when it comes to understanding people and showing empathy professionally, especially when you have a manipulative boss in the workplace.

• Everyone has the ability to be manipulative but can decide not to act on it at work by staying mindful and being candid.

• When you are not sure of whether you are truly being manipulated by an individual at your workplace, it's helpful to check whether you are overthinking your interactions in the workplace.

It is as if you are having a nightmare: Imagine that you have a supervisor in the workplace who is hellbent on doing everything within their power to make life miserable for you, playing with your sanity and emotions. Perhaps this is a fantasy that can be tempting to believe on your worst days at work when you are sitting through meetings that are tedious or rushing to complete tasks to meet deadlines. Despite the hair-pulling and frustration that usually happens with jobs, you don't believe that any boss could be manipulative, right?

You need to understand that manipulation in the workplace is real whether it happens to you or you manipulate others. Even when you manipulate your colleagues at work and believe that you are doing it for the right reasons such as telling them they look good because you are trying to persuade them to help you do something, no real winner exists when you start playing puppeteer. You need to protect yourself against the professional world's string-pullers and learn to cope with manipulation that occurs in the workplace.

# Workplace Manipulation Signs

If you are always voicing all of your thoughts at your place of work, you will get fired from work quickly. You need to understand that professional communication is required in work environments. That means preventing yourself from spreading or sharing unnecessary negativity, such as manipulative behavior, with your peers.

**If your place of work is feeling hostile, uncomfortable, or tense, pay attention and watch out for the following signs that your manager or boss is a manipulative individual:**

● Your manager or boss loves to point out areas where problems exist but they are never interested in doing anything to contribute to finding solutions to those problems: A boss who is manipulative might use your mistakes as a way to belittle you and insult your abilities instead of them to offer you helpful criticism or provide you with helpful idea. When you complete your tasks at work only because of anxiety, it is not healthy or sustainable. A good manager should point out the flaws you have or the areas that you need to improve upon, and they should also let you know ways that you and your colleagues can improve yourselves.

• Your manager or boss is using gaslighting or guilt to keep you motivated: For instance, asking you to take on extra work or staying late at work by convincing you that you are increasing their workload by refusing or that you don't work hard enough. And if your boss agrees to things such as deadlines or time-off requests but then changes their mind later, you need to also look out for similar tactics of gaslighting. When a person denies verbal abuse, it is a sign to pay attention to.

• It always feels difficult when having direct communication with your manager: Sometimes, communication in the workplace can be difficult. We can become tired, stressed, cranky, and so on. But you must ensure that you don't second guess yourself if you are constantly feeling as though your manager or boss is giving you the run-around. Manipulators are experts at withholding insights or details that might make you see their deceptive behavior.

## Reasons for Workplace Manipulation

Manipulation in the workplace does not always happen on purpose. Even when it happens, it is not done with the intention of being malicious. Children quickly get to know which of their parents will likely say yes to them when they ask them for something. They also start paying attention to what causes their parents to say yes or no. Even as children grow older, there is not much difference in other social relationships. You may decide to flatter a colleague at work before asking them later to perform more tasks. Or, if the option is given to you, you may avoid scheduling your performance review at a time that is too early in the morning, before coffee brightens your manager's mood.

This is manipulation that happens in the workplace and it is the clean part of the manipulation. But tendencies of manipulation are linked to dark personality traits that every one of us shares.

**We have seen that the main dark personality traits or the dark triad include:**

• **Narcissism in the workplace:** Being preoccupied with one's future plans, accomplishments, appearance, and self-obsession, is a symptom of a narcissistic personality. However, the individuals who display narcissistic tendencies are not always extroverts who are known to be masters at getting whatever they want. While these people's behaviors can be destructive, the individuals themselves should not be seen as demons. Like every other person, individuals with narcissistic personalities possess light and dark personality traits as well.

• **Machiavellianism in the workplace:** These individuals are usually very manipulative and during social situations, they have a chess player-like mentality. Machiavellians are not more interested in getting attention than narcissists: In their place of work, they are usually more focused on pursuing their goals. And sometimes, they can even do it with little regard for ethics or at the expense of others.

• **Non-empathetic tendencies:** Individuals who have psychopathic tendencies are characterized by emotional responses to stimuli that are blunted, and these individuals may not have a great ability to empathize with other people. As a result of this disconnection from others, psychopaths may behave impulsively, they may behave like Machiavellians, and they may also have little regard for individuals that their actions have affected.

Ensure that you discuss your situation with the HR department of the company if someone is continuously pulling your strings and the situation is getting out of hand, if you are being mistreated, or if you are feeling isolated. Like many other issues that are discriminatory, women and people of color have a higher risk of experiencing coercion or manipulation in the workplace.

While you will not have picture-perfect days every single day, it is important that the work environment is safe and free from manipulation.

# Communication Strategies for the Workplace

Even if you want to manipulate your coworkers so that you can meet the goals of your team and harmonize with your colleagues, manipulation in the workplace can go wrong. If you believe that your coworkers need to be manipulated before you can get along with them in the workplace, you should pay attention to your strategy of communication or switch to a new category of work.

**Instead of flattering your coworkers or using passive-aggressive workplace tactics that lack integrity, you can try doing the following:**

**Being more straightforward with your colleagues:** The sense of fear or guilt that we have after making someone upset may make us try and manipulate or persuade the people we supervise or our coworkers when we need to ask them to do something for us. Be straightforward with them. If you want them to accept criticism, stay late at work, or take a look at an important project, ensure that you are open and respectful. Your colleagues will appreciate your truthfulness and honesty and this will allow you to provide answers truthfully and remove any unnecessary stress you may be going through from your day.

**Evaluating your professional communication style's ethics:** Are you the type who gives other people compliments to make them like you? Do you use guilt as a weapon to make your coworkers assist you? You may use these tactics that do not seem obvious because people usually rationalize their behavior when they are not sure of the right thing to do. While you may have a reason for manipulating your coworkers, it may result in unnecessary problems and harm in your workplace.

If you are not completely sure of whether your manager or boss is manipulating you, check whether you are overthinking the interactions you are having in the workplace. We usually spend considerable energy and time scrutinizing how we or other individuals interacted in conversations that we had previously, in work meetings, or at events. You may be suspecting a particular individual to be manipulating you but they may not be doing anything. Their strange behavior or comment may not be anything, or perhaps they may just be having a bad day. The beauty of professional boundaries is that everyone doesn't have to know. So, give other people space as they are human and need to be able to do what they want to do too.

Manipulation in the workplace is inevitable. Psychopathy, Machiavellianism, and narcissism are qualities that every one of us has and qualities that we may give in to occasionally. Not empathizing with people who are struggling with them as well as the temptation to display manipulative behaviors is hypocritical, even if the person is your manager or boss. However, nobody deserves to be manipulated and exploited in their workplace.

# CHAPTER SIX:
## Spotting Emotional Manipulation in Relationships

Emotional manipulation signs in relationships can sometimes go unnoticed as they can be very subtle. These signs have the ability to make you completely powerless. Manipulation is popular in relationships. Every one of us is capable of manipulating people.

However, when emotional manipulation continues to repeat, it can be a major red flag in relationships and can cause distress to the individual being emotionally manipulated.

How can you know when someone is going through emotional manipulation in a relationship?

Manipulation aims to alter the behavior of the person being manipulated. Every one of us has manipulated one person or the other at some point in our lives. For instance, when you convince your friend to go out with you to watch a movie and skip school on a particular day, that is manipulation at work.

You only tried to convince your friend to skip class and go watch a movie with you, and that doesn't appear to be particularly sinister, you may say. But when emotional manipulation continues to happen in a relationship, it can cause damage to the once-healthy relationship.

When individuals use mind games to try to gain control over you, they are labeled emotionally manipulative people. People usually use emotional manipulation to gain an unfair advantage over their partners or to control them.

It is important to remember that these individuals are not searching for psychological tricks to manipulate others. This might even be unconsciously done, thereby making the manipulator need therapy to manage their issues.

Mutual trust, understanding, and respect are what a healthy relationship is based on.

You might find it hard to spot emotional manipulation as it can be subtle. It can make you feel helpless, misunderstood, and overwhelmed. We will take a look at the signs to look out for if you want to identify emotional manipulation in relationships.

How can emotional manipulation affect a relationship?

Emotional manipulation is capable of turning a relationship that is healthy into a sour one and it is capable of causing damage in the relationship. When wounds are created through emotional manipulation, it can get worse as time passes.

### Emotional manipulation can affect your relationship in the following ways:
- It can lead to an increase in negative communication.
- It can result in low self-esteem.
- It can cause problems in communication as well as misunderstandings.
- It can create feelings of insecurity and a lack of trust.
- It can impact a person's sense of safety.

# Emotional Manipulation Signs

Now, let us discuss some signs of emotional manipulation. We will be looking at emotional manipulation signs that are common in relationships. If you are having feelings of being manipulated in your relationship, you may be right.

## They are always the victim.

The manipulator always acts like they are the victim who is innocent in the story they have twisted to suit them and paint you as the bad guy. You always believe that you are the one who made an error and feel like it is your fault that something is not working well. And you believe that the manipulator is the person who got affected by your mistake.

After some time, you start believing that the version of the story they have told is the correct one as your self-esteem decreases.

## You always meet them at a location of their choice.

Have you noticed that you always meet the manipulator at a location of their choice?

It can be very empowering when you come to see them at their favorite restaurant or at their home. Although they feel comfortable and safe in an environment that is familiar, you are bound to be on edge. You get an unfair advantage from this, thereby causing a power imbalance.

## You always feel misunderstood.

Do you always feel like they don't understand you? Feeling misunderstood is not something new in relationships. Emotional manipulators know how to make you believe the version of the story they are telling without you even realizing it. They thrive where there is chaos and always do things like pitching two people against each other while they watch happily.

If you notice that you are always in the middle of a misunderstanding, chances are that you are being manipulated.

## Your weaknesses can be used as a weapon against you.

This is a key sign that a person is being emotionally manipulated in their relationship.

Suppose you always feel bad after opening up to this individual. Chances are, this person has been using your vulnerabilities and weaknesses as weapons against you and bringing them up whenever you are in the midst of an argument. This can be a huge problem for you.

## You are the one being criticized.

No matter what you do, you always feel like you are not doing enough and your best will never be good enough for the manipulator. This is a key sign of emotional manipulation that happens in relationships.

You always get judged and criticized by the individual and this makes you start to lose faith in yourself and the desire to have a healthy relationship with people starts to fade. It is as if you are always being attacked for little things.

## The manipulator makes you feel like they are the one doing you a favor

A person who is emotionally manipulative volunteers for responsibilities and tasks they have no intention to do and behaves as if they are actually doing you a favor by doing those tasks, only to bring it up during a misunderstanding and use it against you.

For instance, the manipulative individual might say they will make lunch every day only to bring it up later and say something like, "I always make lunch for you but you are ungrateful." They might take you on expensive vacations or buy you gifts and then bring it up later during a misunderstanding as a favor they have done for you.

## All they see is the negatives.

Emotional manipulators find it hard to see the positives. They always see the negatives. For them, the glass is always half empty and not half full. They often have a pessimistic view of life and never cease to find faults in everything that you do.

These individuals have perfected the art of seeing negatives in a good situation.

For instance, if you are excited about a promotion that you received at work, the manipulator would quickly remind you of the additional responsibilities the new position requires instead of being happy about your promotion.

## They never give you the chance to speak for yourself

Do you have a partner who never gives you the chance to answer questions for yourself but speaks for you even before you say a word? One common sign associated with emotional manipulation in relationships is when you have a partner who never gives you the opportunity to share your opinion. The manipulator may invalidate your opinions when they talk to you.

When you are trying to make a point, an emotional manipulator may talk over you and interrupt what you are saying, thereby keeping you isolated from the ongoing conversation.

## Aggression is channeled indirectly.

Passive aggressiveness is a common sign of emotional manipulation. What the manipulator does is to avoid confrontation with the person and then their aggression is channeled indirectly.

When they display inappropriate behavior, they are good at making excuses for their behavior and using silence as a means of punishment. Tools such as snide comments, microaggressions, and so on are also used to take you off balance while they are still being nice to you.

Insults might also be masked as compliments to get you confused. This is something that emotionally manipulative women usually do.

For instance, the manipulator may say something like, "You act so childish and immature sometimes, and it's cute." This confuses you and makes you wonder if they actually hate you or love you.

## Ultimatums are a major part of your relationship.
Is your partner always dropping ultimatums?

You might have a partner who is quick to drop ultimatums and issue threats that they will leave you at every little issue. They don't mind making you feel insecure and anxious and love to have the upper hand in the relationship.

You may notice that you are constantly walking on eggshells whenever your partner is around and this is because of their behavior.

## They make you doubt yourself and have feelings of insecurity.
Have you found yourself beginning to have feelings of security over things that you didn't even care about before?

This is something that happens when there is emotional manipulation in a relationship. Your partner may compare you to individuals they were attracted to in the past or their ex-lovers, they may complain about your weight, and ask you to be like another individual.

All of this makes you start having issues that were never present in your life. If this continues for a long time, you may find yourself having symptoms of mental health problems such as depression and anxiety.

## They always belittle or mock you.
Do you have a partner that makes you feel like you are too small?

They may trigger your insecurities by passing snide remarks thereby making you feel insecure even when you are in the company of people.

They are not bothered about saying something like, "Don't listen to what she is saying; she doesn't know anything about being financially stable." She hates that I look at female models."

Spending time with these people always leaves you feeling drained.

## They are always lying.
Have you ever found it hard to believe your partner because you felt that every word they say is a lie?

An emotional manipulator has mastered the art of lying about big things and small things. They are always lying about little things like what they ate for lunch and things that are more serious like whether they are still seeing their ex.

When an emotional manipulator is involved, you can never tell whether they are telling the truth, and this makes them angry.

## You are always being blackmailed.
The manipulator can say something like, "Do this, or else…"
Emotionally manipulative people usually use blackmail as a weapon to make their victims do what they want them to do. They could issue threats that they will leak your private photos, expose you to your family and friends, and so on to put you back in line. The stress in the relationship may start making you feel like you are stuck in the relationship and have no way out.

## You are facing too much pressure.
You feel like they are always monitoring and watching you and you always find yourself facing too much pressure. Living in a fishbowl is what some individuals call this. The manipulator pressures you into

doing something you would not usually do. It can be something like buying a property or car that you can't afford or getting butt or breast implants.

## They use negative humor to highlight your weaknesses.

They use jokes and humor as a weapon against you and then when you get offended, they say you are over-sensitive. The jokes they crack about you are designed to trigger you and make you react. They enjoy making you lose balance, and you often find yourself wondering why they cracked a certain joke about you, whether it was a subtle attack on you, and what they meant by that.

## Gaslighting is present in the relationship.

One of the popular examples of emotional manipulation is gaslighting. You are sure that a certain incident happened, but the manipulator insists that it didn't happen and you start questioning your sense of reality and sanity.

Your genuine issues and concerns are usually dismissed or minimized, and all of a sudden, you start believing the story the manipulator is telling about how the event played out.

## They always enjoy causing a scene.

People who manipulate others emotionally are not afraid of dragging you into social situations that are uncomfortable for you. They love to yell at you, create a scene even in public places, or shame you in public.

This person even badmouths you to your families and friends while making them believe that they themselves are the victims. They may even come to your workplace. You usually dismiss your feelings because you don't want to create a scene.

**You feel insignificant and never feel good enough.**

You feel like you are insignificant and that you are never good enough for the individual. You also feel that nothing you do will ever make you good enough for them. This person always makes you feel like the ugly duckling in your relationship, and you feel insignificant.

They always talk about your failures in the relationship and highlight them, and your successes are never celebrated.

**You feel like your arguments and feelings don't make sense.**

Emotionally manipulative people use statistics, research, and facts when arguing with you to prove their point. They are brilliant, thereby making you feel like you are fighting facts and statistics. And you may even start feeling like your arguments and feelings don't make any sense. You are being compelled by this tactic, and you begin to question your sanity when you are speaking with them.

# Why Emotional Manipulation?

Most individuals pick up techniques of emotional manipulation from their dysfunctional families, so it is a common thing to see people consciously ask themselves the question of whether they are emotionally manipulative.

Many individuals may not even know that they are emotionally manipulative, as they do it unconsciously. Some people engage in emotional manipulation unintentionally.

**The following is why individuals are emotionally manipulative:**

- They don't have proper communication skills.
- Their self-esteem is low and they need to feel that they are powerful and in control.

- They don't have the social skills that are important for healthy interactions.
- Their emotionally manipulative behavior may be a result of a disorder, such as narcissism, that they have.
- They grew up in dysfunctional families or broken homes.
- Their emotional wounds, immaturity, and pain.

How can you deal with the effects of emotional manipulation?

You need to first identify emotional manipulation before you can deal with it effectively. If you believe that your partner is unintentionally manipulating you, you can discuss the situation with them and ask them if they would like to go for therapy.

If you have a partner who keeps manipulating you despite all your efforts, you may need to rethink your relationship and get help professionally.

# CHAPTER SEVEN:
## Choosing Victims

There is a category of people who attract manipulators. We will look at those traits that attract manipulative people.

Emotional manipulators use dishonest tactics, guilt, and gaslighting to exploit the weaknesses that their partners have and maintain control of the relationship. So, what traits in an individual attract manipulative people?

If you are bothered about why you appear to have many manipulators in your life, you may want to know the exact traits you have or the things you do that draw them to you. You may also be wondering why you are attracted to people who manipulate you.

Why do you seem to be attracted to manipulative friends? First off, you are not the only one with manipulative friends. Many other people also have manipulative people in their lives.

If you notice that you are a magnet for manipulative people and constantly find yourself in relationships with manipulators, then one trait you may have is vulnerability. That may be one reason why you keep being a target for manipulators.

An emotional manipulator is a person who is an expert at influencing their partner's behaviors and feelings to their own advantage.

Manipulators usually use anger, guilt, gaslighting, button-pushing, and other dishonest tactics to exploit the weaknesses that their partners have and stay in control.

This pattern is quite common: individuals who are nice can continually attract people who are manipulative, such as friends and partners, who abuse, exploit, and emotionally manipulate them. Why do nice people often get exploited and manipulated, and why do the same people seem to experience this over and over again?

Could something be wrong with these people?

- No, nothing is wrong with them, even though they continue to find themselves in relationships with people who are emotionally manipulative.
- Yes, they have specific traits that individuals who are manipulative find captivating. Their empathy and vulnerability make them targets for manipulators. They also want to help people and give people the benefit of the doubt.

These are wonderful qualities. However, the manipulator may also be seeing that you wear a label on your chest with a written message that says "Pick me."

You will soon learn to keep the manipulative individuals away if you learn to recognize the traits you have that draw them to you and work on the traits.

## You can become vulnerable to emotional manipulation if you have these traits:

### You lack boundaries or have damaged boundaries.

People who are manipulative are good at targeting individuals that have boundary issues. That means that there is room for a person who is emotionally manipulative to convince you that people who set boundaries are selfish people.

How does an emotionally manipulative person know that you have boundary problems? Individuals who have good boundaries often communicate their boundaries very clearly when they first meet you.

So, how can you fix this?

Set boundaries. Perhaps, setting boundaries is something important that you have to learn to do in life. You can say no and protect yourself when you set boundaries. Boundaries are important for every healthy relationship. So, ensure that you learn to set healthy boundaries and stand by them.

## You love to take care of other individuals.

People who are empathetic love to do things for other individuals, and this is not a bad thing. But when healthy relationships are concerned, we care for individuals, not take care of individuals.

This may be shocking, but most individuals are capable of taking care of themselves even though they may not be experts at it.

Individuals who are emotionally manipulative are willing to play victim to make you give them your attention and take care of them.

So, how can you handle this?

You can fix this by allowing other individuals to take care of themselves. At first, it will not feel very comfortable, but when you notice that another adult has something they are struggling with, ensure that you give them the opportunity to work things out themselves.

Individuals who manipulate people emotionally love to play the victim. So, ignore that and use your energy to take care of yourself instead.

## You are a believer in love at first sight.

Love at first sight looks good in the movies, but the reality is that love takes time. Someone may say they fell in love with someone immediately after the person said hello to them or right from the moment they met the person.

People who are emotionally manipulative like to target individuals with boundary issues. This means that the door is open for an individual who is an emotional manipulator to convince you that only individuals who are selfish have boundaries.

Remember, a person with low self-esteem is more prone to fall for an emotionally manipulative individual's deceit.

So, how can you handle this?
Love takes time to grow. It is developed with understanding, trust, time, and communication. If the person who is manipulating you emotionally is asking you to move in and live with him the same week you met him, you need to think twice.

## Low self-esteem.
You may be telling yourself that everybody has low self-esteem at one time or the other. Although this may happen, this trait of low self-esteem is highly attractive to emotionally manipulative people when an individual has problems with self-love.

You choose a person who unconsciously makes you remember that you have parents who were dysfunctional. When you are not able to love yourself unconditionally, which means loving all the things that are easy to love as well as the things that are hard to love, you may attract to yourself a person who mirrors you.

It would help to know that emotionally manipulative individuals also lack unconditional self-love and have low self-esteem. So, what can be done about it?
You need to work on loving yourself.

Treat yourself the same way you would treat a person who is your best friend. If telling your best friend that he is horrible doesn't seem like a good idea then don't tell yourself that you are a horrible person.

And, of course, you can fake this until it becomes a part of you. You don't need to believe it at first.

## You connect with people who are familiar to you.
Truth be told, no individual likes to feel awkward, uncomfortable, or different. You look for the road that is well-traveled, connecting with individuals who possess characteristics that you are familiar with.

Unfortunately, a lot of times, the familiar is dysfunctional. You may pick a person who unconsciously reminds you of your parents who are emotionally manipulative. If you are able to make the relationship you have with the dysfunctional partner work, you will be able to fix what was broken in you when you were a child.

You like this, right? Sorry, you can only fix problems that you have had from your childhood by working on yourself.

So, how can you fix this?
A therapist can help you out here. They will help you fix any issues you have that are unresolved so that you can stop attracting people who are emotionally manipulative. The traits we have discussed are the traits that make you more vulnerable and attractive to the manipulator.

Understand that being vulnerable is not a bad thing. You just need to ensure that you set healthy boundaries and do your best to protect yourself from individuals who are manipulative because the power to do this is in your hands.

# CHAPTER EIGHT:
## Mind Control

You can make your own idea someone else's idea. When you control someone's mind, you can put your idea into their mind and make it theirs.

This way, you get the person to do your work. People are not sure whether they should do that thing or not. But when you put the idea into their minds, they are able to do it.

You are aware that this will benefit you the most, but you act like it will only benefit other people. Making individuals worried about something is necessary. This happens in online shopping. A product is marketed online to the extent that you feel that you have to buy it at all costs.

Marketers also set a limit. They might say that there are only 50 products remaining, so it will make you move fast to buy them without thinking too much about the product. You will place the order quickly without any idea of how your experience with the product will be. When you do this, you are controlling the minds of people and convincing them to buy your product quickly.

You need to learn two things from this. First, you need to put your idea into the minds of the people and create a need for your product. Second, do not give them the opportunity to think about the decision or the opportunity to focus on any risks associated with the decision.

You can get people to tell you what you want to hear when your idea is already their idea.

Manipulators like to control other individuals just to prove that they are better than those individuals or to get their point of view across. Our thoughts are important and they are responsible for the actions we take. Check an individual's experience, as it will determine their future actions. We may not have complete control over other people's lives, but there are things we can do to get into their minds.

Try to improve yourself to get better instead of keeping other people down. You will feel better when you are improving your life than when you are trying to keep others down for your own advantage. Don't think of how to control someone's mind because you think they will perform better than you. This can also have a negative impact on you. For instance, a person who has an exam to write and is focused on controlling another person's mind because they think the person will perform better than them will only hurt themselves. This is because they will spend time focused on controlling the other person's mind to distract them instead of reading for the exam. This can create more problems for you.

## Steps for Changing Someone's Mind

Is it possible to learn how to change an individual's mind? What techniques of communication work for this purpose? It can be hard to change a person's mind. This is because people often have their ways of doing things and it can be difficult to change the beliefs they hold on to. But good communication can help you with this. Talking to the person and knowing their thoughts can guide you on the right words to say and the right actions to take.

Do you really want to learn how to change an individual's mind? You can achieve what you want without bullying or forcing the person into changing their mind. This way, they will not resent you for making them change their mind.

**You can do the following:**

**1. Start by appreciating them honestly and praising them.**

● When someone is praised for the good things they have done, it is easier for them to listen to things that are not pleasant after they have been praised. If praise is not involved, it means the person is not being appreciated for the good things they have done and anything they are being told to do might appear critical.

● Offer sincere praise. For someone to sound genuine when they offer praise, they have to actually appreciate the person's work.

● The praise you give should not be formulaic. When formulaic praise is given, the person waits for the criticism that is coming.

● Be specific with the praise. Point out the particular things the person did well, instead of being generic and generalizing everything.

● If you are not happy with the work someone has done, you can let them know the areas they have done well in and the areas they should improve upon to perform better next time. This is an effective way to help someone improve. Sincere appreciation makes the person open to receiving your feedback and can be effective when it comes to getting an individual to change their mind and behavior.

**2. Talk about the mistakes you have made before criticizing the other individual.**

● When you admit that you have made mistakes, it shows that you are aware that the task is hard and that the mistakes that the person has made are understandable. This encourages the individual to rise to your level and makes their importance match yours.

● Have the genuine attitude that what makes you perform better is because of the more experience you have which translates to high personal standards that are currently above the capabilities of other individuals.

● This includes the relationship you have with children and entry-level employees. You should not expect a 12-year-old to make the same decisions that you make at age 40. You did not make the same decisions when you were 12.

- When you give unilateral feedback, it gives the impression of a person who is a perfect overlord chastising a follower who is flawed.

A person's importance is diminished.

## Tactics for getting an individual to change their behavior

- "You may have made a mistake, but I have even made worse than you have made. No one was born with the knowledge of everything. Experience is what teaches us, and you are doing better than I was at your age."

### 3. Indirectly call attention to the mistakes individuals make

- When someone makes a mistake, avoid going all out to criticize them for it. You can indirectly call their attention to the mistake they have made. People are usually aware of what they have done wrong, so when you directly call their attention to it, it brings about resistance because it feels like you are issuing an order.
- When you approach someone's mistake indirectly, it gives them the opportunity to make their own conclusion. They are able to save face, thereby allowing them the opportunity to correct the mistakes they have made.

## Tactics for changing an individual's mind.

- Offer sincere praise and then tell them how to improve without pointing accusatory fingers. You can say something like, you have done a great job working hard, and if you focus on adverts, you will increase the number of clients. Avoid saying something like, you have done a great job, but you did not bring in clients.
- This helps you avoid the negativity associated with the feelings of failure.
- If you notice that a person did not do a task well, do the task yourself and then show the work you have done to the person. A proper example of diligence is set by this.

## 4. Make the individual's fault appear easy to correct.

- This is an area that is important when it comes to learning how to change an individual's mind.

## 5. Allow the other individual to preserve their pride.

- People like to feel important. Since they have a craving for importance, if you take away their importance, they will resent you and it will be more difficult to influence them later. Allow people to preserve their pride, even during the times when you are giving them feedback.
- You can allow them to preserve what they care about and their pride.
- If you notice that a role doesn't match a person, focus on the other strengths that the person has and make those strengths shine.
- Accept that people make mistakes out of inexperience or momentary carelessness, and not that they lack the ability.
- Avoid embarrassing the individual who made the mistake publicly. Express confidence in the individual publicly, to preserve their social bonds.
- If you have to let people go, ensure that you express that you are not letting them go because of their work quality, but because the company's needs are changing. Tell them that the business believes in their potential and is rooting for them.

## 6. Give the individual a great reputation to live up to.

- Every one of us loves to feel important. When you are valued for your reputation or for certain traits, it makes you feel important, and you will work to keep feeling important.
- If you have the desire to improve a particular thing about an individual, behave as though the individual already has that trait as an outstanding characteristic that they have.

## Tactics to use.

• If an individual has a poor reputation for the trait that you want an improvement for, it may sound disingenuous if you reverse it. Instead, what you should do is to praise a character trait the person has, and then link it to the person's reputation. For example, an individual may be a hard-working person but may always make mistakes. So, you can praise the individual's diligence, and let them know that they can overcome their carelessness and mistakes if they focus hard.

• You can say this to a customer who is angry: "I have always loved your patience and fairness, and I want you to apply those characteristics in this situation. Please forgive our customer service for their mistakes."

• To an individual who has rejected you: "I have respected you for your open-mindedness and I know you will be willing to reconsider our proposal and change your mind if presented with more information."

• Do this for individuals who have a history of being underappreciated: look for a good trait they have and emphasize it.

## 7. Instead of giving orders, ask questions.

• There are benefits that come with asking questions.

• It gives your partner the opportunity to make their own conclusions on their own. People usually like their own ideas more than the ideas of others.

• It preserves importance, agency, and pride. The individual is following their own orders instead of following another person's orders. This person has ownership in the path forward. Someone can be made to change their behavior this way.

• Your partner's creativity is stimulated. New ideas that are better might actually show up.

## Tactics to use.

- "You might decide to consider this." "What are your thoughts about this?" "Do you think this would work out?"
- Ask your staff when you don't have a clear solution.

### 8. Praise every of their improvement.

- When you praise every improvement, the other individual is inspired to continue improving.
- Don't say, "I'm not good at this. Whenever I praise someone, it stops them from achieving their full potential as praise gives them an early reward." When you declare your goals for your weight loss publicly, you already get some social recognition that you desire and this may make it self-defeating. But you should not let this stop you from praising people for their accomplishments.
- Individuals should know that people crave importance the way they crave food, and when you give them a little importance, it will increase their hunger for more.
- Look back on the events of your life and remember times when your entire future was turned around by a few words of praise. You can praise other individuals and make a positive impact on them.

## Tactics to use.

- Some relationships, especially work relationships and relationships with parents, have changed into a cycle of yelling. You need to break out of this vicious cycle so that you can have healthy relationships.
- Praise should be specific. Instead of simply giving flattering remarks, pick out a particular accomplishment and praise the person for it. This way, your praise sounds more genuine, and it also forces you to look for genuine appreciation points.

# CHAPTER NINE:
## Persuasion: Getting People to Say Yes

One hard task for a lot of individuals is to get someone to say yes. It is not only salespeople that need this skill, we also need it. Knowing how to get a yes from your family, friends, clients, and boss is a skill u need to learn.

Although only a few individuals know how to make someone say yes to their offer, you can learn the right techniques to get any individual to say yes to your offer.

You can apply the techniques we will discuss in your day-to-day life and it can also be used when you have a service or product to sell.

## Influencing with pre-suasion.

The act of influencing your customers' minds and getting them to have a soft spot for your product and be sympathetic about it even before you start talking to them about it is referred to as pre-suasion.

Your success is determined by the words you say right before you deliver the message that makes you successful.

You don't have to say anything. Your customers can even subliminally start falling in love with your product if you create an environment for that. For instance, a person who secured 4 jobs actually said something before the job interviewers started asking them any questions.

When the person asks the interviewers a question like, "What qualities or qualifications did you notice in my resume that made you select my resume?" the interviewers may start focusing on the person's positive qualities.

Here are two more scenarios where individuals said yes as a result of pre-suasion.

The first instance is when an individual went to different shopping malls to ask for the phone numbers of the girls who were passing by. He was not able to collect the phone numbers from the girls. However, he was very successful with getting the phone numbers of girls when he tried asking for their numbers close to a flower shop. In the case of the flower shop, it was successful because it got the girls in the mindset of romance.

In the second scenario, a company that sells furniture changed the background image in their adverts to test the adverts. They used the image of coins in one advert and displayed their furniture on clouds in another advert. People searched for cheap furniture on the company's website when they saw the advert with coins in the background. On the other hand, people who saw the advert with the clouds in the background searched for comfortable furniture when they got to the website of the company. An image is capable of influencing people's minds.

Instead of selling your products directly to the people, you subconsciously get the people to like your product first before you start selling to them.

## Make them like you.

Studies have shown that people feel connected and have a high likelihood of saying yes to people they like. Look for common hobbies, similar values, and shared interests between you and the other individual, and use this tactic to get them to say yes. Spend time and look for genuine similarities that exist between you and the other individual.

## Have a legitimate reason.

Having a reason for why you are making the request is important. It has to be a legitimate reason. Ensure that you use "because." Studies show that people are more likely to say yes to your request when you give them reasons for your request. People might even say yes to a request even if the reason is bizarre.

It is not enough to just give reasons; giving an incentive also helps if your request is very big. You can tell them that you would assist them in their future projects or you can give them a monetary incentive. Ensure that you know why you are making a request before you make it.

## Show your knowledge and expertise.

Ensure that you always talk about your knowledge and expertise before you start telling them the main thing you want to say.

When people become aware that you are a person with a lot of knowledge and experience, they will carefully listen to what you have to say.

Talk about the books you have written, your awards, and your famous clients. If you have a product that you are selling, you can let the people know the number of years your company has been in existence and the number of satisfied customers your company has. This would increase your chances of getting yes. When you show your expertise, it brings about a dramatic change in the way the people you are talking to perceive your data.

## Create scarcity for a sense of urgency.

When you have a product that is displaying a limited stock alert on your website, it can increase your sales. Your sales will be increased as a result of the fear of losing out on the exciting product. Prospects say yes when they have the fear of losing out on exciting opportunities.

Most individuals won't take any initiative unless they see that there is scarcity. The scarcity principle is used by sellers to increase their sales. Have you ever looked at products on an online store and noticed that it has a limited stock or a limited-time discount notification?

The notification creates a sense of urgency in the people's minds and they rush to purchase the products.

Let your audience know what is unique about your product and what is genuinely rare. You will find this same principle helpful and can use it in your day-to-day life.

For instance, if you tell your friend that you will only be free by this Saturday afternoon for the whole month, the likelihood of them joining you will be higher.

In the same way, you can let your colleague know that if they assist you with your project, they would gain new knowledge which would be a great addition to their portfolio. When you create scarcity, you will find it effective in helping you get a yes from people.

## Social proof helps.

Social proof entails sharing testimonials of your product or service to build trust from prospects. Imagine going on a vacation in a country and visiting a new place where you have no idea of the best restaurants to go and eat at. If you find two restaurants, one with 2 people eating and another one full of people, which restaurant will you choose to eat at? I bet you will choose the restaurant that has many people, right? This is what happens when people are purchasing products or services online. They have a high likelihood of purchasing the product or service which has a rating of 5 stars.

A lot of times people make decisions without being aware of the right decision to make. During such times, they follow the decisions of others. In terms of sales and marketing, this is called social proof. It involves making people see the social proof of individuals who look directly like your current prospect.

For instance, if you want to sell an online course to students, you can tell the stories of students whose income levels and age are similar to your prospects.

When you are trying to persuade other people to do something, the idea is to emphasize the fact that a lot of people are also doing that particular thing you want them to do.

## Getting your foot in the door.

This technique is one of the most popular and most effective techniques.

For this technique, you first ask the person for something small before moving on to a bigger request. The small request you make should be something easy and something that many people can easily do. A lot of people use this foot-in-the-door technique. If someone wants to ask for money, they first ask for a small amount and then ask for a larger amount of money after some time.

When you are trying to make sales, you can request that your prospects sign up for a webinar or a questionnaire first then you can pitch the product after that. Ask them to do something small first that makes them committed and then you can later ask them for the bigger thing.

## Label.

Labeling involves assigning a belief, attitude, or trait to an individual before making a request. Ensure that the request that you make is not inconsistent with the label. It should be consistent with it.

If you have a colleague at work who always submits projects late, some of your colleagues may be giving that colleague who is struggling to submit projects on time the wrong labels.

They might say something like, "he can never get any work done" or "he will always be late to submit projects." The individual will lose confidence and end up continuously delivering projects late when he hears his colleagues say such things about him. However, if you tell that colleague that they are dependable and hard-working, they will eventually start submitting projects on time.

Once your colleague submits the project at the right time, ensure that you give him compliments. You can say something like, "I have always known that you are a trustworthy and reliable person".

When you give them compliments, the compliments will motivate them to work harder and deliver on time, and they will do their best to always submit high-quality projects on time.

Sometimes, giving an individual a label is not necessary. Instead of giving them a label, you can encourage them to confirm that they possess desirable traits. This way, you are allowing them to self-label. Make it a habit of genuinely labeling people with the kind of traits that match the request you want to make.

# The reciprocity principle.

The reciprocity principle is a social rule that shows people's willingness to give back to other people when they first receive something from them.

Can you remember the times when your friend or neighbor gave you a beautiful gift? In this kind of situation, there would be a feeling within to return the favor and give them a gift as well.

Companies may use this principle and give people free samples of their products in shopping malls. Studies show that when individuals use a free sample of a company's product, they have a high likelihood of purchasing the product. Reciprocity encourages giving. If you want to get other individuals to say yes to your request, doing something for them first will encourage them to say yes.

When you give someone something or do something for them with an element of personalization, they become obligated to say yes to your request. If you are looking for people to complete surveys, you can send the request with a handwritten message on a post with their name. Doing this will increase the number of people who will complete the surveys because you have taken your time to personalize the letter so it stands out. This encourages people to create time to respond.

Instead of looking for who can help you, get used to asking the question, "Who can I help today?"

# Freedom to accept or reject the offer.

When you make a request, you tell the individual that they are free to either accept the offer you have made to them or to reject it. Many of us dislike it when a person forces us to do something. We want to have the freedom to make any decision we want to make and this is why you should let the other individual know that they can either accept or reject the request.

## Make a plan for implementation.

Even if you persuade an individual to purchase your product online or perform a task, there is a low chance of them actually purchasing the product or performing the task. This is the case because making a promise is different from actually fulfilling it.

Social media has made many individuals procrastinators. So, you need to make a plan for implementation if you want to really commit to doing something. Making a to-do list will not magically make it happen. Commitment is necessary.

When individuals make a concrete plan without stating what task they will perform, when they will perform the task, and how they will perform it, the chances that they will complete the task are low.

Studies show that people usually act on plans when they make concrete plans. A plan that people implement usually has it broken into what, when, and how.

For instance, if you want to increase the exercise you do, you can state clearly that you will go for a run when you return home from work on Saturdays.

When you are trying to persuade other people, ensure that you encourage them to make a concrete plan on a piece of paper with clear details on how they will achieve the goal they want to achieve.

## Give figures and facts and tell stories.

When you are persuading your audience, it is good to share the facts and figures with them. This is a helpful trick in sales. Stories can also be included in your pitch because stories often fascinate people.

Stories transport your prospects to another world. Even politicians are masters at using stories in their campaigns to get more votes from people. Motivational speakers and teachers capture their audience's attention through storytelling. Psychologists say that people get very critical of what they have been told when they are exposed to numbers.

The audience's ability to pick out inaccuracies in what has been presented is usually reduced when you tell a compelling story that connects with them. Remember that it is a human being who will use the product or service you are offering, so ensure that you use a warmer tone when talking to them.

Keep in mind that your product or service would be used by a human being. So, have a warmer tone when you speak to them.

Instead of always using numbers and charts to persuade your audience, ensure that you use pictures of real people. It is easy for people to form a connection with a subject when photos of real people are used.

Studies show that doctors would order more tests, conduct a more detailed analysis of the condition of a patient, and detect more abnormalities if the photograph of a patient was simply attached to a CT scan or an X-ray compared to when the patient's photograph wasn't attached.

This means that your chances of getting yes are increased when you humanize information.

Have a full understanding of the goal you want to achieve and then use a story to bring it to life. Look for characters that your audience can connect to and show their desires and motivation.

## Give genuine compliments.

People often like to receive compliments from others. Humans are self-centered beings. Studies show that individuals have a high likelihood of responding favorably to the request of a co-worker if that co-worker complimented them right before making the request. There are many other studies that showed that when you give genuine compliments to people, it increases your chances of getting a yes from them.

Waiters are often given a bigger tip after giving diners compliments for the way they made a great selection of dishes from the menu.
In the same way, when hairstylists tell their clients that their new hairstyle is so beautiful, they get a bigger tip. Even though many individuals are aware that people often give compliments so that they can get others to do something for them, they still say yes to those people. It is good to give compliments, but you must ensure that you do not overdo it as it will appear fake. Compliments should not be generic.

Before asking anybody to get something done for you, think of something good that the person has done for you and then include a compliment when talking to them.

## End your conversation on a high note.

Have you seen that singers don't usually perform the songs that are the most popular at the beginning or middle of their concerts, but at the end? Singers do this because they are aware that if they don't leave their most popular songs till the end of the concert, their fans will get excited and go home after watching the performance of the most popular song, thereby leaving the concert before it comes to an end. This doesn't mean that first impressions don't matter. First impressions start the conversation so they matter. But it is important that your conversation is ended on a high note. How an experience ends is usually more memorable and important than how it starts.

Do you remember you were having a wonderful presentation until your colleague poured a glass full of water on your laptop? You were having a memorable holiday trip until you had issues with your return flight that got canceled and you had to spend so much looking for a good hotel.

If you pay attention to ending your conversations on a high note and make subtle changes to make it happen, you will have increased chances of getting yes from people. Do your best to save the best news until the end. This way, people will feel the impact more.

So, you can use these strategies to effectively get a yes from individuals. Ensure that you understand your goal first before making a request. When making a request, give them the opportunity to accept or decline your offer, and don't be too pushy.

# CHAPTER TEN:
## Understanding Human Behavior

You need to understand the basics of human behavior to be able to read people's minds. Experiences help people relate well with the world. Your experiences may include replying to an email from work or even something that is as life-changing as giving birth to a child.

Whenever an individual has an interaction with an organization, that individual will have an experience. Whether that experience is transformative, mundane, or even something that is in-between, it will create an emotional response that, in turn, will shape the individual's attitudes as well as inform their future behaviors. Whether it is to stay late at work, recommend the business to friends, or buy more products.

So, there is a need for organizations to know how the experiences of people affect their feelings, thoughts, and actions toward their business if they have the desire to drive profitable behaviors. It is not enough to just recognize this connection. Organizations have a role to play when it comes to actively shaping how individuals process their experiences and how they respond to those experiences by managing the human experience cycle's five elements.

- The experience cycle: The things that actually happen to an individual during an interaction.
- The expectation cycle: What an individual expects will occur during an experience.
- The perception cycle: How the individual perceives their experience based on the expectations they have, which are evaluated against emotion, effort, and success.
- The attitude cycle: What sentiments and opinions a person holds

regarding the organization.

• The behavior cycle: How an individual interacts with a company, which is heavily influenced by the individual's attitudes.

# Formation of Human Behaviors

Although it is important to manage the relationship between emotions, experiences, and actions to develop emotional bonds that are lasting, organizations should also have an understanding of why individuals have the feelings they have and why they do the things they do.

Although humans are quite complicated, this can be a tricky thing. People are not decision-makers who are completely rational and who only act on logic. Our behavior is also influenced by many other hidden factors. Organizations will struggle to consistently create experiences that are engaging if they fail to address these underlying determinants.

Fortunately, everybody shares some characteristics that are fundamental. When organizations recognize the traits that human beings have and embrace those traits, the organizations will be able to make connections that are lasting.

## You need to know the following:

• There are two modes of decision-making that people have: the logical, slow, and deliberate one, and the one that is automatic, fast, and based on mental shortcuts and biases. People mainly use the latter one, which is also referred to as intuitive thinking, when it comes to making decisions, especially when they are in the midst of a crisis or stress. Unfortunately, instead of organizations to cater to people's intuitive side, many organizations spend a lot of time trying to appeal to people's rational side.

• People usually remember things according to the feelings the experience gave them, especially during the end of an interaction and at the most extreme points. When designing experiences, think proactively about the emotions that will likely be generated by the experience during these critical junctures.

- Everybody sees the world through their own personal and unique lens. It is hard to put ourselves in another individual's shoes as a result of this reality. Leaders and employees are more familiar with the products, services, and processes of the company than their suppliers, prospects, and customers. A lack of empathy or miscommunications can be created by these knowledge gaps. You will be able to identify and mitigate resulting issues when you recognize this innate self-centeredness.

- People thrive on positivity and hope and respond well to feeling good about the future. Organizations that are effective motivate the individuals in their ecosystem, and they do this by painting a picture of success that will occur in the future that addresses their individual aspirations and needs.

- People like to form connections with other people who are like them. They usually trust those people that they believe are like them or those institutions that they believe are like them more than they trust others. Understand that the social groups that people belong to are an important area of influence, and look for ways to assist customers and employees in building connections that are meaningful.

- People have four intrinsic needs, such as a sense of purpose, progress, control, and competence, that they strive to fulfill. Instead of putting your focus on extrinsic needs such as price and monetary compensation, you can ensure that you are designing employee experiences and customer experiences that address these intrinsic needs.

There are many theories and definitions of human behavioral research, but generally, it is known as the study of how people interact with each other and how they interact with the environment around them. According to behavioral science, the human brain often relies on mental rules of thumb or heuristics to make satisfactory and swift decisions. However, these heuristics sometimes fail and result in cognitive biases, and they are systematic errors present in our thinking.

When organizations are creating experiences and managing them, they need to anticipate these heuristics and design around the biases and heuristics as they will impact people's behaviors, attitudes, and perceptions significantly.

**While more than a hundred different heuristics and biases have been identified by behavioral research, they can be categorized into six:**

- **The people around us influence us heavily.** This is about one of the six key traits that humans have. Humans are social creatures. As a result, individuals often go with the wisdom of people that they consider to be experts or they go with the wisdom of the crowd.
- **Individuals often prefer simplicity more than complexity.** Individuals often choose the options that they find easier to process mentally, even when an option that is more complicated is the better option. And it also applies to communications. People often like language that is simple and clear more than confusing buzzwords and corporate jargon.
- **Losses affect individuals more than gains.** The decisions we make are not based on the final outcome's rational evaluation, but the decisions are based on an unconscious evaluation of the potential losses and gains of each choice.
- **There is a misjudgment of our past and future experiences.** People often misjudge the past and future experiences that we have. Our memories are like a series of snapshots used to judge our experiences retroactively; they are not videos looping in our heads. We also struggle to make predictions that are accurate regarding future events or ourselves.
- **Individuals make decisions that are dependent on**

**context.** Decisions that individuals make are based on context, such as how a decision is framed, the unconscious priming effects that an individual encounters, the physical environment in which the individual makes a decision, or other available choices for comparison. Decisions that individuals make are not made in a vacuum.

- **The current emotional and visceral states of individuals affect their actions.** People's behaviors are influenced by how they are feeling during an experience. For instance, individuals act more impulsively when they are hungry. They rely more on intuitive thinking when they are experiencing emotions that are strong. Being aware of this can assist you in taking steps to defuse customers who are angry before requesting that they process a statement that is logical, such as a solution to their situation.

Organizations will be able to build stronger emotional ties with their audience, which will lead to higher profits and stronger loyalty when the organizations are able to create experiences that show how people actually think and behave instead of treating people like completely logical, rational thinkers.

# Understanding the Behavior of Humans

Understanding the behavior of humans is many people's desire. There are individuals who love to look for typical patterns of behavior and also the common causes of destructive and unusual thinking and behavior. What makes human beings self-sabotage? What makes people commit suicide when it is not in line with our struggle for survival? It appears many people are only concerned about themselves so they take advantage of others to get what they want.

**You need to know the following:**
**1. Many don't believe in themselves.**
If everybody had more self-belief, this world would be filled with

less negativity and more positivity. No matter the self-doubt, people would grab opportunities, live their lives to the best of their abilities, and achieve more. When you make unfavorable comparisons to others, you believe that other people are better than you, and your self-belief decreases.

## 2. Everybody has a fear of something.

Every one of us fears something. It could be a fear of being alone or something like a phobia of spiders, which is an irrational fear. Fear promotes wasted opportunities. It paralyzes people. Often, the event is not as bad as the fear, but for those individuals who give in to the fear that they imagine, the fear stays in place.

## 3. Many people feel misunderstood.

Have you ever felt like you were standing on the outside and looking in? If you have, you are not alone. Many individuals have times when they feel misunderstood and alone. They have feelings of being somehow different from the billions of people that exist in the world. There will always be a person somewhere in the world who feels the same way as you do. This means that we are never really alone. Other people understand you more than you think they do. There is something universal that connects us all together, and this underlying universal understanding is something you may not be aware of.

## 4. Denial does not fix the problem.

People have learned different ways to justify their own behavior and fool themselves. Some people may physically abuse their partner and then justify it saying they don't understand how people cheat on their partners. Isn't it quite interesting to see someone justify physical violence but find deceit and lies in relationships appalling? There are individuals who tell themselves stories that are fake and that are not the reality yet this is done with the intention of coping with reality. Unfortunately, if you are thinking that denial fixes the problem; it doesn't. if you want to resolve anything, you need to first acknowledge the existence of that thing.

## 5. Our parents play a huge role in our success.

Our parents are important when it comes to the success we achieve later in our lives. Although we have total control over our lives as adults, our upbringing plays a crucial role in whether we become successful or not. It is important that we understand how our upbringing may help us or hinder us in life so that we can know what to do to get the most out of our lives. Many parents are not aware that they play a key role in the future of their children, emotionally, mentally, and spiritually.

## 6. Everybody wants to have peace of mind.

Everybody desires peace of mind but they don't know how to find peace of mind. You need to separate yourself from the noise of the world, avoid comparing yourself to others, and then find your own path if you want to have peace of mind. What do you desire to achieve while living here on earth? What do you consider important in your life, and are you having time to do what you consider important? When you allow too much external influence, your focus is diluted and you may lose your way and peace of mind.

# CHAPTER ELEVEN:
## Standing Your Ground

It is possible to deal with a manipulator and put them in their place. Ideally, a person will notice a manipulator and then run far away from them. But there are times when you cannot run away from them.

Sometimes, the person manipulating us is our colleague at work or our boss. Other times, the person is our adult child, spouse, or family member who uses manipulation tactics to get what they want from you and other members of the family.

Things become complicated. For these situations, some techniques exist that you can use to disarm the manipulative people in your life.

**Here are the techniques:**
**1. Call the manipulator out.**
One way to disarm a manipulative individual is to call them out. Let them know that you are aware of what they are doing.

If an individual is trying to bait you into an argument that you know you cannot win or if they are gaslighting you, you have the power to decide not to participate.

**Here are some things you can say:**
- "I am not going to discuss anything that is not relevant to this conversation."
- "We cannot talk if it won't be possible for us to honestly discuss this."
- "I think you are saying this to start an argument that will lead to a fight, so I am putting an end to this conversation."
- "You are asking for extra work that we didn't agree to from the

beginning. Why would I do the extra work?"

Once you say something like any of the above, it doesn't mean that the manipulator will suddenly leave you alone. It is unlikely that they would do that.

Manipulative individuals will fire up their tactics when they are faced with resistance, but that is what will make you know that you are taking back your power from them. Manipulators dislike it and will often lash out, but if you stand your ground. They won't be able to take advantage of you.

## 2. Reset the conversation.

One common tactic that manipulators use on their victims is to encroach on their personal space. When this person is having a conversation with you, they might move too close to you. They might try to give you a pat on the shoulder or back to make it more difficult for you to reject them.

When a person is trying to make you do something you don't want to do by using physical proximity, take a step back so that you can reset the conversation.

## 3. Maintain eye contact.

Manipulative individuals are good at asserting their dominance and getting what they desire by using eye contact. This is called the hypnotic gaze. It is when an individual focuses on you intensely, and it is designed to test boundaries.

Make them have a taste of their own medicine. This may require some practice, especially if the manipulative individual is aware of what to do to throw you off your game. You need to practice and master how to remain calm when a manipulator is trying to use eye contact to throw you off balance.

If you believe an individual is trying to use intimidation to manipulate you, say no to their request and ensure that you maintain steady eye contact in the process. If you want to put the manipulative person in their place, ensure that you make eye contact.

## 4. Respond with emotional neutrality.

Manipulative individuals are experts at weaponizing emotions for their own advantage. If they have a way to make you angry, ashamed, feel guilty, or get you worked up, they can use your vulnerability against you.

You need to remain neutral when dealing with the manipulator who continues to push your buttons. This is one way to disarm them.

This might require every ounce of strength, but you must ensure that you get the emotion completely out of your response and then leave instead of reacting in an emotionally explosive way.

- "I am not interested in following you to that place, so I am hanging up the phone."
- "I don't agree with what you think of me, and I will be leaving now."
- "I am sorry that you think this way. I am done with this conversation."

When you immediately take away access from this individual for as long as you need, this is when neutrality works best. That way, you will be able to take time to process everything and determine whether you want to proceed with this person or not.

## 5. Don't give manipulators an opportunity.

Refuse to give individuals an opportunity to make you their target for manipulation. If you have a colleague at work who likes to help you a little so that you can do something they want you to do for them, you can refuse to accept their help. You can say, "No thanks. I can manage on my own."

## 6. Boundaries are important.

You need to set boundaries, especially when dealing with people who are manipulative and whom you cannot easily separate yourself from, like your parents, grown children, coworkers, or siblings.

When we set boundaries, they protect us from individuals and things that affect our ability to work in healthy ways. The situation determines the kind of boundaries to set.

### Here are some examples:
- You might refuse to talk about issues that always end in arguments.
- You might say that you will no longer lend money and put an end to conversations that have to do with finances.
- You might tell an individual that you won't respond to their text messages or answer their calls when you are at work or after a particular time of the day like 10 pm.

Be clear about the boundaries you have set and also be confident. When setting your ground rules, ensure that you use "I" statements instead of "you" statements.

"I won't be lending you money anymore. I am your friend, but not your bank."

The manipulator will resist, but as you stay consistent and firm, things will change. This does not mean that the manipulator will change, but it means that you will no longer be facing the same drama you used to face before.

## 7. Try the technique of fogging.

The technique of fogging is used in assertiveness training. You can use the tactic to deflate a situation and handle an individual who is aggressive toward you.

Look for the kernel of truth present in whatever the individual is saying to you, acknowledge it, and then after acknowledging it, move on from the conversation.

This way, you are able to address the parts that are true without engaging in the parts of the criticism against you that are not true or the exaggeration.

## Fogging works this way:

**Colleague:** You failed to enter our office meeting into the time tracker.

**You:** Yes, you are right; I forgot.

**Colleague:** You don't always remember to do this, and it messes up our schedules.

**You:** I didn't remember today and I understand the impact it has on the tracking of our data.

**Colleague:** This is ridiculous. I should not have to ask you weekly for time tracking.

**You:** You had to ask me today, and I can see that it is frustrating.

When using the fogging technique, ensure that you stay emotionally detached and calm in the face of aggression.

This strategy is quite effective because you are not allowing yourself to be drawn into an argument or engaging with the exaggerated parts of the conversation.

The energy of the situation is deflated by this but you remain firmly rooted in the truth in this scenario. You never accept the parts that are not true.

For instance, in the scenario that we talked about above if it is only three out of ten times that you have forgotten to enter the tracking information, it means that your colleague is simply being hyperbolic.

Nobody says you should agree with things your colleague said that

are not true, but what you can do is acknowledge the part that is true: which is that you forgot today.

## 8. Make the manipulator to be specific.

Manipulative individuals are masters at weaponizing generalizations. This can be something like pointing an accusatory finger at you that you are always doing damaging things to them.

Ask the person for examples, then after asking, turn it back on them. If a person accuses you of always doing something to them, ensure that you ask them to prove it.

"Can you give me some examples of some things that I have done so that we can fix the issue?" This might get them frustrated.

## 9. Everything should be documented.

This point is especially important in any situation that could have legal implications in the future or in professional settings. If you are aware that you are dealing with an individual who is manipulative, and who has a knack for gaslighting and dishonesty, then you need to document everything.

Write down everything that was said, when you had the conversations, and get everything documented. This is excellent if you need to have proof of their behavior, and you are also protected against the game of "who said what" that these manipulative individuals usually play.

## 10. Avoid getting isolated.

Manipulative individuals do their best to keep you dependent on them professionally, financially, emotionally, romantically, or any combination of these. They do this by isolating you from your family and friends.

Knowing that you are not spending enough time with your loved ones and close friends is the first step to take towards breaking free

from the grip that a manipulator has over you.

## 11. Don't give the manipulator what they want.

Individuals who are abusive often feed off negative emotions and they also know exactly what to do to push buttons to get a response from their victims. When you see this coming, don't take part in it.

If you know that a call from a family member will be filled with lies or drama, you can ignore the call.

If they continue to call and you make up your mind to speak to them, don't give room for things to turn toxic. You have the power to tell a person, "I am not going to do this particular thing, and I won't change my mind about it."

## 12. Use calm persistence.

This technique is a skill that is also known as "calm persistence." You continue repeating your main point or saying what you want over and over without raising your voice tone or getting angry.

It involves unwavering and staying calm in the face of manipulation. You stand by your message and refuse to become pulled into an argument or a conversation that is sidetracked.

Suppose you are planning an outing with a friend who is attempting to pressure you into spending a large amount of money on a more expensive option.

Your friend: "We should spend the entire time at the Resort. We will have a great experience."

**You:** "I would prefer we go to a place within our budget."

**Your friend:** "But give it a second thought. The amenities and the beautiful views. We should not miss this once-in-a-lifetime opportunity."

**You:** "It looks great, but I would prefer we go to a place within our budget."

**Your friend:** "You are always playing it safe. Won't you like to make some beautiful memories?"

**You:** "I understand what you are saying, but I would prefer we go to a place within our budget."

**Your friend:** "I will make up for the difference. Let us enjoy the best and you can pay me back much later."

**You:** "I appreciate the nice offer you made, but I would prefer we go to a place within our budget."

In the scenario above, the friend who is hypothetical is trying different ways to make you accept choosing the more expensive option. When you continue to repeat your main point and you keep saying that you want to stay within your budget, your friend will eventually get the point and stop asking.

Manipulation involves control and power. You will be happier when you are able to take back your power and control of your life from the manipulator. Although we have discussed helpful strategies, it is important that you also get support when needed.

It is not your fault that you are being manipulated. Don't consider yourself a weak individual if you find it difficult to employ some of these tactics, especially if you are using the strategies against loved ones.

If you find yourself feeling trapped in a manipulative relationship, see a professional for counseling or help. A trained therapist can guide you and help you with strategies that are specific to your situation.

# CONCLUSION

Do you have a partner that creates unreasonable rules that you must follow? If they set impossible deadlines that you must meet, if your bathroom breaks and mealtimes are strictly regulated, and you have no access to your friends or your own money, then you are being manipulated.

When your partner, who is the manipulator, is doing all they can to make you follow a strict set of rules by taking all your decisions away from you, it can be frustrating. This prevents you from thinking for yourself, and when you are not thinking for yourself, it becomes easier for the manipulator to implant their own agenda.

You may have been putting up with this for a long time, but this does not have to go on forever. You can prevent people from controlling your mind. If you notice that someone is manipulating you, you have to break free from their grip and their attempts to manipulate you.

We have talked about the steps you can take in this book. If you want to break free from the manipulator's grip, you need to follow what we have discussed.

Remember to remain in close contact with your family and friends because a manipulator can isolate you from your family and friends so that they can have total control over you. They might take you to their own location where they have all the power. Refuse to allow the manipulator to stop you from seeing any of your family members or friends. If they insist on preventing you from seeing your family members and friends, don't listen to them. You must insist on seeing your family members and friends. And if the manipulator still says no, you can walk away.

Refuse to put up with the manipulator's sulky or moody behavior. Treat that behavior with disdain, and don't fail to tell them that the behavior is childish and immature and you won't put up with such behavior.

You can tell what a person is thinking by checking for their pain points, and you can do this by asking them the right questions. You need to establish a personal bond with someone to be able to know what they consider valuable.

When having a conversation with someone, you have to be a good listener and not someone who talks more than you listen. You can't be talking non-stop without really paying attention to understand what the other individual is saying. That is not how to have a conversation. Poor communication is something that affects relationships a lot, and a manipulator might be a poor communicator. So, you need to work on having effective communication with them.

Sometimes, you will want to know what is on someone's mind before you say anything to them. This can help you say the right words and do the right thing. Saying the right words can help you close business deals and develop relationships that can last for a long time. If you want to know what is on someone's mind, you need to study their body language and follow the steps we have discussed in this book.

What triggers an individual's emotions? Where is the individual's comfort zone?

You need to give the person a chance to speak. Don't be the only one speaking non-stop. If you want to form a connection or get people to take action and purchase your products or services, you can do it. Ask questions that are open-ended questions that give the individual the chance to share their challenges and strengths. You can also share stories about the things you have done for other people. People will often acknowledge if they have the same issue when you share your story with them, and this can help you better understand their needs.

It can help to consider personalities. Observe the qualities an individual has to determine what they consider important and who they are as a person.

Someone may be very analytical and relate well with people when they come prepared and methodically lay out their ideas. They may prefer that people be prepared to use numbers to back up their initiative. And if a person comes to them but doesn't do that, then the person may lose the opportunity to win them over.

You can search for clues into a person's personality by paying attention to verbiage and characteristics. An individual who likes to be dominant, for instance, might have a handshake that is overly firm. Sarcasm will often be inserted into a conversation by individuals who welcome humor. You can determine their approach and their values by using these clues.

Nonverbal communication helps with mind reading. Don't forget to pay attention to body language clues as nonverbal behavior is important.

If a person leans in, it means they are engaged in the conversation. If they turn away, look down, or back up, it means that they are not relating to whatever you are telling them.

You can also get clues from a person's tone of voice. For instance, if a person is responding to you in monotone, it means that they are most likely not interested in what you are saying and they are not attached to your concept. If the person looks at you and moves closer to you when you speak, it means that they are finding what you are saying valuable.

We have said that you should pay attention and be a good listener. Ensure that you listen to what a person is saying, and also listen to what the person is not saying. While this is more difficult when the conversation takes place over the phone, a voice that is passionate or engaged is obvious and cannot be hidden. It also shows when a person is frustrated.

You will hear a sigh or the person's tone will change. Developing a good ear that has the ability to listen for subtle sounds is important.

Avoid communicating by email anything that involves emotion or that is critical. You can make a phone call instead. Emails can make it hard to be perceptive and they are hard in conveying what the words mean.

The ability to change the mind of an individual when they already have their ways of doing things is an elusive skill. You may find it frustrating when you are unable to convince someone to see things from your point of view. Even when you are sure that what you are doing is the right thing.

A lot of the things we do to change an individual's mind do not work as well as intended. Many of us have received training on the wrong ways to influence people. This is what makes us have little success when it comes to persuading people. New studies in behavioral sciences tell us what makes the old ways futile.

We need to put an end to using our gut instincts to change the minds and attitudes of people, including their logic, reasoning, and aggressive selling because they usually don't work. We need to use a different approach.

But things get easier and clearer once you understand how individuals make their decisions. You will see a positive and noticeable change in how your suggestions are viewed by people. You will discover a surprising willingness and less resistance and they will say yes to you.

It can be hard to change a person's mind. Studies show that people argue with us more when we reason with them. Our efforts are spent on people's rational minds and this makes them resist us and argue with us more.

The good thing is that there is now an easy and reliable way to change the minds of people. A complicated approach is not needed to convince people to accept your view of something. You can win people over through some easy solutions that help to align their subconscious minds with you.

You can change someone's subconscious mind. It will initially be hard to focus on people's emotions. Our instincts make us give reasons for the choice or option we bring. This will hurt your chances at changing the minds of people so it is important that you suppress this urge.

You will engage someone's conscious mind if you rationalize with the person. And their conscious mind is not in charge of their decision-making. When you get a person subconsciously aligned with you, it will be easier to get them to do what you want them to do. They will easily say yes to you if you do this well. When you give the person reasons why they should listen to you and do what you ask them to do, the person will be moved to change their mind and be in agreement with you. Mastering the art of human psychology is not something unattainable. You can achieve it with practice and it will help you to become more successful in life.

Made in the USA
Las Vegas, NV
13 May 2024

89800103R00125